ROAD TO
RELATIONSHIP

PRAYING THE WORD | THE PROPHETS

The Road to Relationship
Praying the Word | The Prophets
By Riley Martin

Copyright © 2023 R2R Relationship

Paperback ISBN: 979-8-9860083-1-8

All rights reserved. No portion of this book may be reproduced in any form without permission from Riley Martin.

Cover Design by Dallas Cole

Printed in the United States of America

CONTENTS

Foreword..5

Introduction..7

Isaiah..9

Jeremiah..102

Lamentations......................................139

Ezekiel...143

Daniel..168

Hosea..192

Joel..208

Amos...218

Obadiah...222

Jonah...226

Micah..239

Nahum..243

Habakkuk..245

Zephaniah...249

Haggai...252

Zechariah..258

Malachi...265

FOREWORD

An accomplished Hebrew rabbi once taught that one of the most beneficial blessings in your life's study will be to learn from the life of the Bible prophets: "Elias was a man subject to like passions as we are" (James 5:17). The biblical prophets taught us many valuable nuggets of truth, but the greatest revelation is that these men were not above us; they were in many ways like us! To follow the prayer life of the prophets is to identify with those who, though flawed in their humanity, teach us about the marvelous mercy of our heavenly Father.

I am amazed at the vision and passion of Riley Martin to dedicate himself to such a great task. I know Riley personally, and I believe the Lord has anointed him for a great work. He even partners with me in prayer for the United Nations Ministry. This book by Riley Martin is a great inspiration and testimony to what God has planned for the next generation. I am sure *The Road to Relationship* series is going to help us today and in future generations enter into that high place in prayer.

Art Wilson, Pastor
The International Church of Metro Detroit
Good Will Ambassador to the United Nations

INTRODUCTION

The prophetic books are powerful because these men of renown wrote under the inspiration of the Spirit of God. Their writings spanned four centuries, from about 800 BC to 400 BC, when the divided kingdoms of Israel and Judah were in a dark period. The prophets spoke to nations and kingdoms, rulers, priests, pastors, and common people, urging them to renew their relationship with Jehovah, their Savior. Although the prophets' messages came straight from the mouth of God, their words were often rejected; consequently, many of the prophets battled mental, physical, spiritual, and emotional trials. Nevertheless, they pursued their mission with everything they had.

These prayers from the prophets represent the darker seasons of our lives. No, not all the writings are despairing, yet as you read through these prayers recognize that you sometimes seem to be driving into the dusk. The road to relationship may pass through desolate, dark terrain. You may be in a dry Ezekiel 37 season (the inspiration for the cover of this book). But just hold on. Set your face like flint, as the prophets did. Because the darker the night, the brighter the light. And when morning dawns, joy will come! If this is your night season, turn on your headlights and keep pursuing the Road to Relationship with Jesus Christ.

ISAIAH

Isaiah 1:2–4

Hear, O heavens, and give ear, O earth: for the LORD hath spoken, I have nourished and brought up children, and they have rebelled against me. The ox knoweth his owner, and the ass his master's crib: but Israel doth not know, my people doth not consider. Ah sinful nation, a people laden with iniquity, a seed of evildoers, children that are corrupters: they have forsaken the LORD, they have provoked the Holy One of Israel unto anger, they are gone away backward.

As we enter into the prophetic books, we find that many of the Israelite community began to turn away from God, which seriously hindered their journey on the road to relationship. Paul indicated there was lust for evil things, idol worship, pagan revelry, sexual immorality, grumbling, and complaining. Paul wrote, "These things occurred as examples to keep us from setting our hearts on evil things as they did" (I Cor. 10:1–11, NIV). If we want to make progress on the road to relationship, we should heed the prophets' messages to God's people.

Isaiah was an eighth-century BC prophet who lived in Jerusalem during the reigns of Uzziah, Jotham, Ahaz, and Hezekiah. His ministry spanned forty to fifty years. He expressed the Lord's disappointment, grief, and anger that his people had forgotten about him and turned to other gods. The Lord's people reacted similarly to Isaiah's messages as they did to the messages of the other prophets: they acted like they didn't care.

Even though the Lord agonized over Israel's betrayal, he still assured his people that if they would return to him, he would forgive them and accept them. He also showed Isaiah the glorious future that awaited his people.

The book of Isaiah is filled with prayers about consecrating ourselves and refusing to turn away from God. Therefore, as we begin turning the pages of this book, we are going to pray a prayer of consecration with a request that God will make us aware if we are ever turning away from him.

Lord, I consecrate myself to you. I pray that if I ever begin to turn away from you that you will send a man or woman of God to correct me. Help me to hear their voice and obey.

Isaiah 1:7
Your country is desolate, your cities are burned with fire: your land, strangers devour it in your presence, and it is desolate, as overthrown by strangers.

Over the years stranger and foreigners—Aram, Edom, Philistia, and Assyria—had invaded the Promised Land and, through assimilation, had corrupted the Israelites' culture and religion.

Our mission and purpose are to bring people into the kingdom of God. However, when "strangers" come in, they should not stay strangers for very long. They should begin to adapt to the kingdom of God in worship, attitude, and spirit. If you notice that strangers are affecting your church culture in a negative way, then something is wrong. You should not allow influences in your life that are not of God. Notice that I didn't say ungodly people should not be in your life. They inevitably must be. But you are to be the influencer, not they.

God, I pray that others will come into your kingdom through the testimony of my life. However, I pray against strangers who would try to destroy or even water down the godly culture you desire for your church.

Isaiah 1:10–16

Hear the word of the LORD, ye rulers of Sodom; give ear unto the law of our God, ye people of Gomorrah. To what purpose is the multitude of your sacrifices unto me? saith the LORD: I am full of the burnt offerings of rams, and the fat of fed beasts; and I delight not in the blood of bullocks, or of lambs, or of he goats. When ye come to appear before me, who hath required this at your hand, to tread my courts?

Bring no more vain oblations; incense is an abomination unto me; the new moons and sabbaths, the calling of assemblies, I cannot away with; it is iniquity, even the solemn meeting. Your new moons and your appointed feasts my soul hateth: they are a trouble unto me; I am weary to bear them. And when ye spread forth your hands, I will hide mine eyes from you: yea, when ye make many prayers, I will not hear: your hands are full of blood. Wash you, make you clean; put away the evil of your doings from before mine eyes; cease to do evil.

This passage is about hypocrisy—claiming to have moral or religious standards or beliefs while failing to live according to those claims. The Israelites had turned away from God and were living sinful lives, but they continued to bring sacrifices to God. They were "practicing" their religion like nothing was wrong.

This would be similar to a person attending church every Sunday and midweek service, but then living in sin throughout the rest of the week. That is a dangerous and scary place to be.

Isaiah's efforts were not to condemn God's people, but rather to bring conviction. Condemnation says, "I've messed up. It's time to give up on God." Conviction says, "I've messed up. It's time to repair my relationship with God." Let conviction motivate your relationship. Cease from evil and God will wash you and make you clean.

God, wash me from any hypocrisy. Help me to cease from doing evil in my life. I want my prayer to be heard and my sacrifices to have meaning.

Isaiah 1:18–19
Come now, and let us reason together, saith the LORD: though your sins be as scarlet, they shall be as white as snow; though they be red like crimson, they shall be as wool.
If ye be willing and obedient, ye shall eat the good of the land.

Remember that neither conviction nor condemnation feel good at first. But we must recognize the difference. The enemy is against us and will use condemnation to make us angry at the word of God, the pastor, or even God himself. But the Lord says, "Come now, and let us reason together." He wants to spend time with us. His correction is meant to draw us closer to him. He desires to cleanse us so that we are white as snow and pure before Him. And verse 19 says that if we are willing and obedient, God will give us the good things of the land.

Lord, I give you free rein to reason with me and show me what I need to do. Then, after I have obeyed and my heart and my spirit are clean, I pray that you will bless me according to your word.

Isaiah 2:2

And it shall come to pass in the last days, that the mountain of the LORD's house shall be established in the top of the mountains, and shall be exalted above the hills; and all nations shall flow unto it.

Much of the language in Isaiah can be classified as double fulfillment prophecy. Like the other prophets, Isaiah's inspired messages had both short-term and long-term fulfillment. Isaiah preached to his generation, but his prophecies also applied to future generations. This double fulfillment will become more evident when we reach Isaiah's prophecies concerning Jesus.

This verse begins, "In the last days . . ." Isaiah's message to the Israelites was that in the last days God would rule the nations from Jerusalem. His house would be established, and all nations would flow unto it.

But we are living in the last days too, so this prophecy applies to our time as well. Pray that this will happen—that our churches will be exalted and experience a massive multinational revival.

God, I pray over every local church that is preaching the truth. Let them be exalted in their community. I pray over your church in this world. Exalt your church in this hour so that all may come to it and receive salvation. Establish your house upon the mountaintops!

Isaiah 3:9–10

The shew of their countenance doth witness against them; and they declare their sin as Sodom, they hide it not. Woe unto their soul! for they have rewarded evil unto themselves.

Say ye to the righteous, that it shall be well with him: for they shall eat the fruit of their doings.

Have you ever noticed that some people who walk away from truth and the church often do it in a grand way? They don't hide their sins, but rather put everything out in the open and blame God. This is nothing new. The backslidden people of God did the same thing in Isaiah's day. But verse 9 basically echoes the old saying "What goes around comes around." Evil people will get their just reward as surely as the righteous will get their just reward. Therefore, don't fear or worry when others attack the church or leave flaunting their sin. God is the judge.

Lord, I pray for those who turn away from you. I will not gossip about them or be envious at their prosperity (Psalm 73:3). I will maintain my integrity and remember that you and you alone are a just judge.

Isaiah 5:12–16

And the harp, and the viol, the tabret, and pipe, and wine, are in their feasts: but they regard not the work of the LORD, neither consider the operation of his hands. Therefore my people are gone into captivity, because they have no knowledge: and their honourable men are famished, and their multitude dried up with thirst. Therefore hell hath enlarged herself, and opened her mouth without measure: and their glory, and their multitude, and their pomp, and he that rejoiceth, shall descend into it. And the mean man shall be brought down, and the mighty man shall be humbled, and the eyes of the lofty shall be humbled: but the LORD of hosts shall be exalted in judgment, and God that is holy shall be sanctified in righteousness.

The end is not great for those who do not regard the work of the Lord. The English Standard Version says, "Sheol has enlarged its appetite and opened its mouth beyond measure." This is both scary and sad. The number of people on this planet who don't regard, believe in, trust, honor, or fear God seems to be growing at a rapid rate. Nevertheless, verse 16 says that in the end God will be "exalted in justice" and will show himself "holy in righteousness" (ESV).

I rebuke the plan of hell to capture the souls of men and women in this world. I pray that people will turn to you as the only holy, righteous, and exalted God.

Isaiah 5:20

Woe unto them that call evil good, and good evil; that put darkness for light, and light for darkness; that put bitter for sweet, and sweet for bitter!

Isaiah wrote this message to the people of his day, but it applies to today's world too. In our culture, evil is called good and good evil; darkness is called light and light darkness; bitter is called sweet and sweet bitter.

Do a quick comparison of the things the Bible teaches against and the things the world celebrates, as well as the things the Bible celebrates and the things the world denigrates. The world is more fascinated with oppression than it is with liberty. It celebrates sinful lifestyles that statistically lead to mental, emotional, and physical trauma. All the while it attacks the church, saying the church is placing people in bondage. That's why I believe Isaiah 5:20 is an accurate representation of today's world.

As Christians, we must not be confused by this sly twist in the world's perspective. We can avoid confusion by knowing what is in our Bibles. Going to church on Sunday is not enough. Get into the word of God every day of the week. Live a better life by following its teaching. Pray the word of God. Don't give in to what society tells you is good or bad. Know it for yourself. Find godly leaders and follow them.

Guard against being deceived by the world, because it can happen. No one is exempt. Hell's mouth is gaping wide, wanting to swallow anyone who falls in its trap, especially those who are seeking to go deeper in Christ. You will not have to fear destruction if you know the difference between good and evil according to the word of God.

Lord, I will not let the world define my outlook on what is good or evil, dark or light, bitter or sweet. Rather, I will rely on your word and let it speak into my life. Your word is perfect and applicable to all generations.

Isaiah 6:1–8

In the year that king Uzziah died I saw also the Lord sitting upon a throne, high and lifted up, and his train filled the temple. Above it stood the seraphims: each one had six wings; with twain he covered his face, and with twain he covered his feet, and with twain he did fly. And one cried unto another, and said, Holy, holy, holy, is the LORD of hosts: the whole earth is full of his glory. And the posts of the door moved at the voice of him that cried, and the house was filled with smoke. Then said I, Woe is me! for I am undone; because I am a man of unclean lips, and I dwell in the midst of a people of unclean lips: for mine eyes have seen the King, the LORD of hosts. Then flew one of the seraphims unto me, having a live coal in his hand, which he had taken with the tongs from off the altar: and he laid it upon my mouth, and said,

Lo, this hath touched thy lips; and thine iniquity is taken away, and thy sin purged. Also I heard the voice of the Lord, saying, Whom shall I send, and who will go for us? Then said I, Here am I; send me.

I remember hearing this passage as a kid and feeling the mystery, awe, and majesty of this scene in God's throne room. The imagery is of a majestic, almighty God who is seated on the throne, and his train, or robe, fills the temple. In that culture, the longer the king's train, the more might he had. Angels were in the room, ready to do the Lord's bidding, and the air was hazy with smoke from the glory of God (cf. Rev. 15:8).

This is a polar opposite to the setting of destruction that Isaiah lived in. What was Isaiah's response to this powerful atmosphere? He recognized that he was not worthy to be in the presence of God. Compared to the Lord, he was unclean and needed to repent. And God granted him repentance.

Today's culture has all but lost a fear of the Lord. It seems that at times we take God's forgiveness for granted. We must not lose our sense of awe and respect toward the One who is seated on the throne. A powerful presence of God should bring us to our knees in repentance.

After Isaiah was forgiven, God asked, "Whom shall I send?" Isaiah immediately rose up and said, "Here am I; send me." Repentance does not lead to sulking, brokenness, or defeat. Instead, it prepares us for commission.

Lord, I stand in awe of your majesty and power as you are seated on the throne. I repent before your presence and pray that you will forgive me. Wash away my uncleanness, and if you can see anything in me that you can use, Lord, here I am. I am fully yours.

Isaiah 7:14
Therefore the Lord himself shall give you a sign; behold, a virgin shall conceive, and bear a son, and shall call his name Immanuel.

The Jews needed an immediate savior. They feared the fierce anger of the "smoking firebrands" referred to in verses 4–5. King Ahaz was thinking of seeking an alliance with Assyria when Isaiah told him the enemies' plans would never come to pass (v. 7) and that Ahaz should ask God for a sign. Ahaz refused, but Isaiah gave him the sign anyway: a virgin would conceive and bear a son whose name means "God is with us." It is interesting that this promised child "never makes an appearance in [the rest of] Isaiah's text or plays a role in the immediate events. This suggests the total fulfillment of the prophecy was outside the scope of the book and looks forward to one who was, as His name implies, truly a 'prince of peace'" (Apostolic Study Bible).

From this verse we give thanks to God for sending his son, Jesus, who became our Immanuel, God with us.

Jesus, I am overwhelmed that you would leave your heavenly throne, be born of a virgin, and become my Savior. Your Incarnation made you sensitive to the feelings of my human infirmities, and provided a way for me to be close to you. Thank you from the bottom of my heart!

Isaiah 9:6
For unto us a child is born, unto us a son is given: and the government shall be upon his shoulder: and his name shall be called Wonderful, Counsellor, The mighty God, The everlasting Father, The Prince of Peace.

Isaiah never would have applied the five "names" mentioned in this verse to an earthly king; therefore, this prophecy was unprecedented! The child announced in 7:14 "would be credited with attributes that belong to Jehovah alone" (Apostolic Study Bible). In our next few prayers, we will focus on the five names of God. (These names appear in the Tabernacle Prayer in the first volume of this series, *Genesis to Job*.)

Wonderful: We praise God because he is wonderful. When you experience the things God does in your life, you can't help but marvel at his greatness—he is so great that it is beyond human comprehension!

God, I praise you because you are wonderful! You amaze me in every way. You are the greatest. You are the only God, and I marvel at you.

Counselor: This is probably my favorite attribute to pray about. As you journey on the road to relationship, you will realize that God is your best counselor. When you don't know the next step to take, talk to God about it. When you need advice on a situation, ask him for it. When you just need to unload some frustrations, he will listen. But make sure that when you talk to him, you also listen for his response, then follow his leading in prayer. In this portion I pray that God will counsel me, my day, and my every step. I pray that he will counsel my church, my pastor, and my family. I pray that I will gratefully receive godly counsel because I want to be close to God, my Counselor.

Jesus, you are my Counselor. I pray that you will lead me, guide me, and counsel me. I pray that you will use me to counsel others by your Spirit.

The Mighty God: God is powerful! Nothing is more powerful than he, because there is no other god beside him. No matter what situation you are facing, it cannot resist the power of God. God is more powerful than the worst evil in the world. Praise him for his power! Ask that you can walk in that power.

Praying this verse should both humble us and empower us. We receive his power because we are with him. All power is in the name of Jesus.

Lord, I give you glory because of your power! I feel so humble approaching you because you are the mighty God. In you I live and move and have my being. Help me, Jesus, to go forth in the power of your might. (See Acts 1:8.)

The Everlasting Father: I first learned the Tabernacle Prayer from Evangelist Josh Herring. I'll never forget him telling me that there were days when he couldn't get past praying about the everlasting Father. He would pray for children of abused homes, children in orphanages, lost souls, and broken families. He would pray, "Lord, I ask that you would be an everlasting Father to them." The reality is the Father is there for you, for me, and for them. He died on a cross to save us all. And whether you need a father in your life or you are seeking to be that comfort to someone else, we need the everlasting Father.

Lord, I pray for all those without a godly father. I pray that you would be a comfort to them. Lead them to a

place of your presence where they can receive fullness of joy. In Jesus' name.

The Prince of Peace: While I do love praying about the Counselor, it doesn't get much better than the Prince of Peace. I don't believe it to be any coincidence that this is the last title. Why? Because once you know that he is wonderful, it gives you peace. Once you have a relationship with the Counselor, you receive peace. When you serve the mighty God, you live under peace. The everlasting Father brings comfort and peace like no other. God is a God of peace. We live in a world where peace is a rare commodity. It is only through Jesus that every individual will experience true peace.

Lord, I ask for your peace that passes all human understanding. I pray for peace when I'm in the valley and on the mountaintop. Let me be content in every circumstance, for I know you are the Prince of Peace.

Isaiah 10:27
And it shall come to pass in that day, that his burden shall be taken away from off thy shoulder, and his

> *yoke from off thy neck, and the yoke shall be destroyed because of the anointing.*

Isaiah prophesied to the wicked people of Israel, telling them that the day would come when the anointing would lift their burden, and their yoke of bondage would be destroyed. The word "anointing" is an interesting word that is found throughout the Old and New Testaments. It translates literally as *fat* or *oil*. It is like the excess blessing that signifies the favor of the Lord. Isaiah declared this favor would one day be bestowed upon the Israelites. Verse 20 (NLT) says the favor will rest upon a remnant who will "faithfully trust the Lord, the Holy One of Israel."

Stay in truth and the anointing will come! Stay in truth and the Lord's favor will come! Don't be dismayed. Your burdens will be lifted and your yoke of bondage will break. The favor of the Lord is yours if you remain in truth.

Lord, I will remain in your truth as long as I live. I pray that your anointing will break every burden and yoke of bondage in my life.

Isaiah 11:1–2

And there shall come forth a rod out of the stem of Jesse, and a Branch shall grow out of his roots: and the spirit of the LORD shall rest upon him, the spirit of wisdom and understanding, the spirit of counsel and might, the spirit of knowledge and of the fear of the LORD.

I have a storied relationship with Isaiah 11:2, dating from 2016. I was a young preacher who was privileged to travel briefly in California with Evangelist Josh Herring. My life was changed when we visited a church in Merced and walked into the office of Pastor Sam Emory. At this point I was unaware that I was standing before an apostolic giant. In the quick ten minutes before service, he shared his story of forsaking a lifestyle of drugs. He showed us pictures, and that testimony alone was inspiring. Then he explained that God had called him even though he had very little education. Finally, he shared a little piece of revelation from the word of God that blew my mind. We then walked into the auditorium, the power of God moved in the service, and many were baptized that day.

On the drive home I asked Josh Herring, "How did this man of God receive such knowledge? What did he do to open himself to these revelations?" The evangelist responded, "I asked him the same questions last week. He said he prays that the seven spirits of Jesus in Isaiah 11:2 would be upon him every day."

I had read this verse before, but I never understood it in that light. From that day forward, for the next two to three years, I prayed that the Spirit of the Lord, the spirit of wisdom and understanding, the spirit of counsel and might, and the spirit of knowledge and fear of the Lord would infuse my life.

I believe those prayers have impacted me in more ways than I will ever discover. Over time, it placed my mind in divine alignment. It is a constant journey, but this was my first step. To be honest, I had always wondered what was the difference between knowledge and wisdom, counsel and might.

Fast-forward to 2022 when I was privileged to be on a Zoom call with Pastor Tim Zuniga, who began the session by reading Isaiah 11:2. I sensed the Lord was drawing me back to praying this verse, so I was laser focused. Pastor Zuniga explained the seven spirits in a way I have never heard. Here is his explanation.

The Spirit of the Lord is the fire that gives us desire. It is a place where we don't have to seek out the Spirit because the Spirit is resting upon us; it is homey and comfortable and normal to live in the presence of God.

The spirit of wisdom helps us see things from God's perspective, which in turn helps us make right decisions. When we are unsure of what decision to make, we tune out self-confidence and listen for the voice of God. Once the Lord speaks, we tune up our confidence to block out all doubt.

The spirit of understanding is about leading. The sons of Issachar understood the times and knew what to do. Without a spirit of understanding you will use old thinking for new opportunities. We are not to lean on our own understanding, but on God's.

The spirit of counsel helps us give on-the-spot counsel or advice to others. It may not provide all the answers to life, but it allows us to know what to do next. The clearest person in the room is the one who will lead, so aim to give clarity and counsel to others.

The spirit of might enables us to continue. Too many leaders are burning out. Do not be weary in well doing. Wait on the Lord and he will renew your strength.

The spirit of knowledge has to do with our thinking. We make decisions based upon the things we know. Knowledge gives power and confidence. God's knowledge allows us to know things we may not have experienced yet. This knowledge is creative, deep, and provides solutions to problems.

We have discussed the fear of the Lord throughout this series. The fear of the Lord is reverence for God. Pastor Zuniga asked me questions like "What do you fear? Is it failure? Criticism? Doubt?" Whatever you fear will be your driving force. If God is your number-one priority, all other fears will fall by the wayside. When we are walking in these attributes, we can hear God say "well done" every day.

These prayers are a prophecy of Jesus Christ. He is the Branch that Isaiah said would grow out of the roots of Jesse. These spirits are mentioned again in Revelation 1:4, and may be referring to the fullness and/or attributes of the Holy Spirit.

Praying these powerful prayers will lead you to a better life. Most important, praying these prayers will expand your mind because it is in divine alignment.

Lord, I pray that these seven attributes would be in my life today: the Spirit of the Lord, the spirit of wisdom and knowledge, the spirit of understanding and counsel, the spirit of might, and the fear of the Lord. In Jesus' name.

Isaiah 12:1–3
And in that day thou shalt say, O LORD, I will praise thee: though thou wast angry with me, thine anger is turned away, and thou comfortedst me. Behold, God is my salvation; I will trust, and not be afraid: for the LORD JEHOVAH is my strength and my song; he also is become my salvation. Therefore with joy shall ye draw water out of the wells of salvation.

Repentance turns away the anger of God. As soon as you repent, God becomes your comfort and strength; you have no reason to be afraid in his presence. The last verse of this passage speaks to me most:

"Therefore with joy shall ye draw water out of the wells of salvation." The Lord is a never-ending wellspring of life. He will save you from your sin, your pain, and your hurt. His Spirit is like a river of living water. Go to him with joy!

Every day I will come to your well of salvation with joy. Lord, you are my life.

Isaiah 14:1–3

For the LORD will have mercy on Jacob, and will yet choose Israel, and set them in their own land: and the strangers shall be joined with them, and they shall cleave to the house of Jacob. And the people shall take them, and bring them to their place: and the house of Israel shall possess them in the land of the LORD for servants and handmaids: and they shall take them captives, whose captives they were; and they shall rule over their oppressors. And it shall come to pass in the day that the LORD shall give thee rest from thy sorrow, and from thy fear, and from the hard bondage wherein thou wast made to serve.

I'm writing to the ones who feel like strangers coming to Christ. Maybe you were bound in a lifestyle of sin. Maybe you walked away from God for a time. Maybe you are coming to God and entering a church for the first time in your life. This passage is for you.

Isaiah wrote, "People from many different nations will come and join them there and unite with the people of Israel" (14:1, NLT). This gospel message is for everyone, not just those who grew up in the church. From the Old Testament to the New, God's plan has always been for everyone.

Isaiah prophesied that you can claim this for yourself: "The Lord [will give] his people rest from sorrow and fear, from slavery and chains" (v. 3, NLT). When you come to God, you don't have to work to repay him for a life lived in sin. This compassionate Master will free you from the cruel taskmaster and remove your chains. He will take your hurt, even the hurts you suffered because of the choices you made, and he will give you rest.

Lord, you are so good. I pray that you would take the sorrow, the fear, and the bondage of my past and

allow me to walk in the rest and peace that you have given.

Isaiah 19:22

And the LORD shall smite Egypt: he shall smite and heal it: and they shall return even to the LORD, and he shall be intreated of them, and shall heal them.

In chapters 13–23, Isaiah entered into a discourse of judgments against many of the nations because of their wickedness. However, in my eyes, Isaiah 19:22 captures the very essence of God's nature: Isaiah said the Lord would strike Egypt and then bring healing. The Egyptians would turn to the Lord, and he would hear their pleas and help them.

God's plan has never been that of destruction but always redemption. (See 2 Pet. 3:9.) He desires for the whole earth to be healed. It is, of course, our choice, but through everything that happens, God is working toward redeeming this world.

Lord, our world is being destroyed by sin. I pray that you will turn the hearts of the people toward you so

they can be healed. Heal our land, Lord. (See 2 Chron. 7:14.)

Isaiah 24:15

Wherefore glorify ye the LORD in the fires, even the name of the LORD God of Israel in the isles of the sea. From the uttermost part of the earth have we heard songs, even glory to the righteous.

According to the footnote in the New English Translation, the phrase "the fires" can be interpreted "in the region of light," or the east. Isaiah coupled this with the phrase "isles of the sea," or seacoasts. Thus, the two phrases refer to all the earth (www.biblegateway).

The rendering of verses 15–16 in the Living Bible is significant: "Hear them singing to the Lord from the ends of the earth, singing glory to the Righteous One! But my heart is heavy with grief, for evil still prevails and treachery is everywhere."

You don't have to be extremely observant to notice this world is full of trouble. Evil and treachery are running rampant. Does this mean you should give up because it looks like evil is winning? No! When you are in the midst of a fiery trial, glorify the Lord! I know that is easier said than done, but that is the way of the Christian life. We glorify his name at all times.

Lord, I will glorify you in the midst of my trial. When it seems as though I'm walking through the fire, I will lift up your name and sing praises.

Isaiah 25:1–4

O Lord, thou art my God; I will exalt thee, I will praise thy name; for thou hast done wonderful things; thy counsels of old are faithfulness and truth. For thou hast made of a city an heap; of a defenced city a ruin: a palace of strangers to be no city; it shall never be built. Therefore shall the strong people glorify thee, the city of the terrible nations shall fear thee. For thou hast been a strength to the poor, a strength to the needy in his distress, a refuge from the storm, a shadow from the heat, when the blast of the terrible ones is as a storm against the wall.

We live in a decaying world. Conditions are like those described in Isaiah 25: mighty cities are heaps of ruins;

cities with strong walls are turned to rubble. We have no control over what everyone around us will do. The actions of the godless will result in the destruction of this world. But in the worst of times, we still exalt God and praise his name. God will be a strength to the poor and needy in distress. He is a refuge from life's storms.

Lord, my world is decaying quickly. I understand that destruction is coming, but I pray that you will be a strength to me in these last days. I will be one of the strong ones that continues to praise you. You are my refuge in the storm.

Isaiah 25:8–9
He will swallow up death in victory; and the Lord GOD will wipe away tears from off all faces; and the rebuke of his people shall he take away from off all the earth: for the LORD hath spoken it. And it shall be said in that day, Lo, this is our God; we have waited for him, and he will save us: this is the LORD; we have waited for him, we will be glad and rejoice in his salvation.

I love these double fulfillment prophecies concerning Jesus. Isaiah may not have had this purpose in mind when he wrote these verses, but Jesus is the fulfillment of Isaiah's prophecy. Jesus has wiped away the tears from our eyes and swallowed up death in victory. Thank him for his salvation!

Jesus, thank you for swallowing up death forever. Your victory makes me victorious every day. Wipe the tears from my eyes, Lord, then I will rejoice in your salvation!

Isaiah 26:2–4
Open ye the gates, that the righteous nation which keepeth the truth may enter in. Thou wilt keep him in perfect peace, whose mind is stayed on thee: because he trusteth in thee. Trust ye in the LORD for ever: for in the LORD JEHOVAH is everlasting strength.

The gates are open to the righteous, and everyone who keeps the truth can enter in. So, above all things, keep the truth! Don't let anything turn you aside from trusting in the truth of the word. Keep your mind stayed on truth. God is your everlasting strength. So, though you may feel weak now, you will receive strength in the end. Just keep on holding to the truth.

Lord, I will keep your truth at the forefront of my mind and in everything I do. I will constantly pray for truth and thank you for truth. I pray that I will stay in this truth through good times and hard times. Your truth is my fortress.

Isaiah 26:8–9

Yea, in the way of thy judgments, O LORD, have we waited for thee; the desire of our soul is to thy name, and to the remembrance of thee. With my soul have I desired thee in the night; yea, with my spirit within me will I seek thee early: for when thy judgments are in the earth, the inhabitants of the world will learn righteousness.

When you truly desire the Lord, it does not matter what time of day or night it is. It might be early; it might be at night. Learn to recognize the drawing of the

Spirit. The Spirit can draw you to pray at any time. Desire to be led by the Spirit in prayer.

Lord, I give you free rein to draw me to prayer at any time. Lead me where you want me to go at the right time. I desire to be close enough to you so I will recognize when you want to talk with me in prayer.

Isaiah 26:16–18

LORD, in trouble have they visited thee, they poured out a prayer when thy chastening was upon them. Like as a woman with child, that draweth near the time of her delivery, is in pain, and crieth out in her pangs; so have we been in thy sight, O LORD. We have been with child, we have been in pain, we have as it were brought forth wind; we have not wrought any deliverance in the earth; neither have the inhabitants of the world fallen.

This passage describes a certain type of prayer called travail. Isaiah likened it to a woman in painful labor, trying to bring forth a child. A prayer of travail feels like something is being birthed in you, and it often comes from a painful situation either in your life or through someone else's life. Travail often leads to intercession, which produces results.

When you feel this type of prayer coming on, don't back away. Be aware that God is birthing something in you, or he is using you to pray for a certain situation. It may be a hard, tough, agonizing prayer, but the end result is worth the pain.

Lord, I will travail in prayer and birth the promise you have placed inside of me.

Isaiah 28:11

For with stammering lips and another tongue will he speak to this people.

Isaiah 28:11 is yet another double fulfillment prophecy. In Isaiah's context, the prophet was offering the northern kingdom of Israel a message of comfort, but they ignored it. Instead, they complained that Isaiah was speaking to them as if they were little children learning their ABCs. Isaiah then warned of a coming storm; the Assyrians—people who spoke a strange tongue—were about to conquer the Israelites and teach them a harsh lesson.

In the New Testament era, we see another fulfillment of this prophecy in Acts 2, when the Holy Spirit was poured out on the Day of Pentecost and the people spoke in tongues. The Lord speaks to his people through tongues. This could be through tongues and interpretation, as outlined in 1 Corinthians 12, or through our own personal prayer in tongues. We should desire to pray in tongues and allow God to speak to us and through us. (See Eph. 6:18; Jude 20; Rom. 8:26–27.)

Lord, I will pray in the Spirit by speaking in other tongues. Speak to me and through me, Lord.

Isaiah 29:13

Wherefore the Lord said, Forasmuch as this people draw near me with their mouth, and with their lips do honour me, but have removed their heart far from me, and their fear toward me is taught by the precept of men.

This verse describes what we would call "going through the motions." The Israelites were praising God with their lips, but their hearts were not in it. Our heart should be at the center of our worship. The expression will come out through our lips, but it must start in our heart.

God, help me not to be so distracted by temporal situations that I merely go through the motions of worshiping you. I want to be aware of your presence and worship you with all my heart. Let my words be an expression of the true worship that is in my heart.

Isaiah 29:24
They also that erred in spirit shall come to understanding, and they that murmured shall learn doctrine.

The prophet Isaiah was "very dissatisfied with [the] attitudes in Samaria" (*Zondervan Bible Commentary*). A "wayward spirit" had led to Israel's deportation after being conquered by the Assyrians.

Christians who question sound doctrine are erring in their spirit. I believe we need to pray this verse over Christianity worldwide. We need to pray that people will come to understand and learn sound doctrine. Also, pray that you personally will seek to know and understand the Lord and cling to sound doctrine. (See 1 Tim. 4:6, 16; 2 Tim. 4:3; Titus 1:9.)

Lord, I pray that all those who err in their spirit and question biblical teaching will come to know and understand sound doctrine. I pray that all will come to a knowledge of the truth, even if this applies to me, Jesus.

Isaiah 30:20–21
And though the Lord give you the bread of adversity, and the water of affliction, yet shall not thy teachers be removed into a corner any more, but thine eyes shall see thy teachers: and thine ears shall hear a word behind thee, saying, This is the way, walk ye in it, when ye turn to the right hand, and when ye turn to the left.

Lord, let Isaiah's words be an answer to prayer for someone reading this book right now.

You may feel as though you have no direction, that you're eating "the bread of adversity" and drinking the "water of affliction" (TLB). God is bringing you through hard times. My message to you is to hold on, because your teacher is going to show up. It may be the Holy Spirit, as described in John 14:26. It may be your pastor or mentor. If you've wandered off the path, you will hear your teacher say, "This is the way, walk ye in it."

Pray this verse! Receive the direction the Lord has for your life.

I pray that Isaiah 30:20–21 will come to pass in my life and the true teachers in my life will come to the forefront. Give me discernment to recognize who these teachers are. Let me hear your voice of direction showing me the right path, and I will walk in it. In Jesus' name.

Isaiah 35:4–10

Say to them that are of a fearful heart, Be strong, fear not: behold, your God will come with vengeance, even God with a recompence; he will come and save you. Then the eyes of the blind shall be opened, and the ears of the deaf shall be unstopped. Then shall the lame man leap as an hart, and the tongue of the dumb sing: for in the wilderness shall waters break out, and streams in the desert. And the parched ground shall become a pool, and the thirsty land springs of water: in the habitation of dragons, where each lay, shall be grass with reeds and rushes. And an highway shall be there, and a way, and it shall be called The way of holiness; the unclean shall not pass over it; but it shall be for those: the wayfaring men, though fools, shall not err therein. No lion shall be there, nor any ravenous beast shall go up thereon, it shall not be found there; but the redeemed shall walk there: and the ransomed of the LORD shall return, and come to Zion with songs and everlasting joy upon their heads: they shall obtain joy and gladness, and sorrow and sighing shall flee away.

What a passage! It can be spoken in a literal or spiritual sense. To those who are fearful and weak, I speak faith and strength! God will heal. God will deliver. God will make a way—the highway called "The way of holiness." Those who walk on this highway will be joyful. Trust in the Lord. He is coming to your desert place.

Lord, I will speak faith to those who are fearful. To those who are sick or bound by sin, I declare your healing and deliverance. To those who are lost, I declare your direction. Your road is the way of holiness. I will receive the joy and gladness you have for me, in Jesus' name.

Isaiah 36:11–21

Then said Eliakim and Shebna and Joah unto Rabshakeh, Speak, I pray thee, unto thy servants in the Syrian language; for we understand it: and speak not to us in the Jews' language, in the ears of the people that are on the wall. But Rabshakeh said, Hath my master sent me to thy master and to thee to speak these words? hath he not sent me to the men that sit upon the wall, that they may eat their own dung, and drink their own piss with you? Then Rabshakeh stood, and cried with a loud voice in the Jews' language, and said, Hear ye the words of the great king, the king of Assyria. Thus saith the king, Let not Hezekiah deceive you: for he shall not be able to deliver you. Neither let Hezekiah make you trust in the LORD, saying, The LORD will surely deliver us: this city shall not be delivered into the hand of the king of Assyria. Hearken not to Hezekiah: for thus saith the king of Assyria, Make an agreement with me by a present, and come out to me: and eat ye every one of his vine, and every one of his fig tree, and drink ye every one the waters of his own cistern; until I come and take you away to a land like your own land, a land of corn and wine, a land of bread and vineyards. Beware lest Hezekiah persuade you, saying, the LORD will deliver us. Hath any of the gods of the nations delivered his land out of the hand of the king of Assyria? Where are the gods of Hamath and Arphad? where are the gods of Sepharvaim? and have they delivered Samaria out of my hand? Who are they among all the gods of these lands, that have delivered their land out of my hand, that the LORD should deliver Jerusalem out of my hand? But they held their peace, and answered him not a word: for the king's commandment was, saying, Answer him not.

The southern kingdom of Judah was under attack! The fearsome Assyrian army had besieged Jerusalem. Sennacherib's chief of staff stood and loudly taunted the people of God who were peering at him from the safety of the wall. Then things got interesting.

Three of Hezekiah's emissaries, Eliakim, Shebna, and Joah, stepped forward and asked the Assyrians to speak in their own language so the Jewish people wouldn't understand their threats and be afraid. The Assyrians responded, "No way. We want everyone to be afraid!" Then the man roared, "Don't believe your king when he says God can save you. He cannot! None of the gods of other nations we have conquered were able to save them, and your God is no different!"

The enemy will try to speak to you through your thoughts and emotions. He will taunt you and tell you, "God won't be able to deliver you. Others just like you have fallen, and you're going to fall too." But the devil is a liar.

What did the Jews do? Verse 21 (NLT) says, "But the people were silent and did not utter a word because Hezekiah had commanded them, 'Do not answer him.'" No matter how loud or how long the enemy ranted, the Jews did not respond. When the enemy comes to you and tries to intimidate you, sometimes the best way to shut him up is to just ignore him. Then his empty threats (his threats are empty because he is lying) will have no effect on you. The King has your back, and he is always victorious.

When the enemy tries to use my thoughts and feelings to speak lies against me, I will choose not to respond to his threats. Jesus, you are my King and you are victorious. You will help me to withstand the enemy and bring me out of my situation in victory.

Isaiah 37:33–35
Thus saith the LORD concerning the king of Assyria, He shall not come into this city, nor shoot an arrow there, nor come before it with shields, nor cast a bank

against it. By the way that he came, by the same shall he return, and shall not come into this city, saith the L%%%. For I will defend this city to save it for mine own sake, and for my servant David's sake.

Hezekiah wasn't sure what to do about the Assyrian threat. Kings from other lands were telling him that surrender was the only way to survive. Thankfully, Hezekiah did the right thing; he sought advice from the prophet Isaiah. Isaiah told Hezekiah that God himself would defend the city and deliver his people.

That is exactly what happened. The angel of the Lord killed 185,000 Assyrian warriors, and the survivors limped home in defeat. Jerusalem was spared.

When you're facing a great trial, you will hear input and advice from a lot of different people. However, stick to the advice of the man or woman of God in your life. Stick to the advice of those with a prayer life. Trust in the Lord and his word, and he will deliver you.

Lord, I will trust your word in the greatest trials of my life. I will seek counsel from your ministers. And I know that you will deliver me.

Isaiah 38:1–5

In those days was Hezekiah sick unto death. And Isaiah the prophet the son of Amoz came unto him, and said unto him, Thus saith the LORD, Set thine house in order: for thou shalt die, and not live. Then Hezekiah turned his face toward the wall, and prayed unto the LORD, and said, Remember now, O LORD, I beseech thee, how I have walked before thee in truth and with a perfect heart, and have done that which is good in thy sight. And Hezekiah wept sore. Then came the word of the LORD to Isaiah, saying, Go, and say to Hezekiah, Thus saith the LORD, the God of David thy father, I have heard thy prayer, I have seen thy tears: behold, I will add unto thy days fifteen years.

We learn from this passage that it is possible to change the mind of God. Isaiah came to the king with devastating news: "Hezekiah, you're going to die." The king turned his face to the wall and wept, pleading,

"Lord, I'm not ready to die. Please extend my life." What happened? The Lord changed his mind and extended Hezekiah's life another fifteen years.

Hezekiah is known as one of the few good kings of Judah. He had a close enough relationship with the Lord that his prayer caused God to amend his plan. I want that type of relationship, where God really listens to my prayers.

God, I want to have the same kind of relationship with you that Hezekiah had. Draw me close to you, Lord, and let my prayers be fervent and effective in your kingdom.

Isaiah 40:3–5
The voice of him that crieth in the wilderness, Prepare ye the way of the Lord, make straight in the desert a highway for our God. Every valley shall be exalted, and every mountain and hill shall be made low: and the crooked shall be made straight, and the rough places plain: and the glory of the Lord shall be revealed, and all flesh shall see it together: for the mouth of the Lord hath spoken it.

John the Baptist was the fulfillment of Isaiah 40 (cf. Luke 3:4–6). I believe this prophecy extends to our day. The world we are living in is a wilderness. We know that God is coming soon. What are we to do?

Our job on this earth is to prepare for the Lord's return—prepare ourselves, prepare others, and prepare the land. We prepare through prayer, preaching, teaching, and studying his word. Our preparation will set the stage for the second coming of Jesus Christ.

God, I will prepare for your turn. I will be the voice crying out in the wilderness, saying, "Get ready! Jesus is coming soon!"

Isaiah 40:8
The grass withereth, the flower fadeth: but the word of our God shall stand for ever.

Lord, thank you for your everlasting word! It is my foundation and my life.

Isaiah 40:29–31

He giveth power to the faint; and to them that have no might he increaseth strength. Even the youths shall faint and be weary, and the young men shall utterly fall: but they that wait upon the LORD shall renew their strength; they shall mount up with wings as eagles; they shall run, and not be weary; and they shall walk, and not faint.

Yes, Christians sometimes grow weary physically, spiritually, and/or emotionally. The enemy swoops in to take advantage of this weakness, especially in young people who haven't had much experience in waiting on the Lord. But those who do learn how to wait on the Lord will be able to soar like an eagle.

Why did Isaiah point to the eagle as an example? "An eagle rises to great heights, but has no jet engine behind him. His body is designed to maximize the power of the air, and he soars on unseen currents with agility and ease" (Allie Boman).[1] The

---

[1] Allie Boman, "What Does 'Wait on the Lord' Really Mean?" https://www.biblestudytools.com/bible-study/topical-studies/how-do-we-wait-upon-the-lord.html

eagle's dependance on the power of air currents is not a weakness; it is the eagle's greatest strength.

Paul wrote, "I take pleasure in infirmities, in reproaches, in necessities, in persecutions, in distresses for Christ's sake: for when I am weak, then am I strong" (2 Cor. 12:10). Your dependence on the Lord is your greatest strength.

Waiting on the Lord is not an exercise in passivity and inactivity. Waiting on the Lord involves action, a focusing on God's power and ability to help in your situation. It entails searching the Scriptures for passages pertinent to your situation. It means thinking about how God has helped you in the past and reminding yourself that nothing on this earth lasts forever. In his own time, God will arrive on the scene with help, strength, and victory.

God, teach me to wait on you. I pray that you will strengthen me in my youth so that I may soar like the eagle, run and not be weary, and walk and not faint. In Jesus' name.

Isaiah 41:9–10

Thou whom I have taken from the ends of the earth, and called thee from the chief men thereof, and said unto thee, Thou art my servant; I have chosen thee, and not cast thee away. Fear thou not; for I am with thee: be not dismayed; for I am thy God: I will strengthen thee; yea, I will help thee; yea, I will uphold thee with the right hand of my righteousness.

The Lord chose you "from the ends of the earth, and called [you] from its farthest corners" (ESV). How do you know you are his "called" servant? Because you are seeking a deeper relationship with him. So fear not! God will strengthen you, help you, and uphold you. He is your strength in time of need. He is your God.

Lord, you have chosen me and I am completely yours. I pray that you will strengthen me in my time of need. In Jesus' name.

Isaiah 42:1

Behold my servant, whom I uphold; mine elect, in whom my soul delighteth; I have put my spirit upon him: he shall bring forth judgment to the Gentiles.

I desire to be God's elect, his chosen one, someone in whom God has placed his Spirit and in whom he delights. As indicated in 41:9, God searches to the ends of the earth and calls people to him. However, "Many are called, but few are chosen" (Matt. 22:14). Just because someone is invited to God's kingdom doesn't mean he or she will end up there. It takes both the drawing of the Spirit (John 6:44) and the person's decision to follow Christ.

If you desire to be one of the elect, how do you go about it? Spend time with the Lord in prayer and in his word. Show him you care about his kingdom. And you will find yourself among God's elect.

Lord, I desire to be a part of your elect. I want to delight your soul, Lord. Place your Spirit within me so that I can do the work of your kingdom.

Isaiah 42:6–9

I the LORD have called thee in righteousness, and will hold thine hand, and will keep thee, and give thee for a covenant of the people, for a light of the Gentiles; to open the blind eyes, to bring out the prisoners from the prison, and them that sit in darkness out of the prison house. I am the LORD: that is my name: and my glory will I not give to another, neither my praise to graven images. Behold, the former things are come to pass, and new things do I declare: before they spring forth I tell you of them.

This is a powerful passage! First, God says, "I have called thee in righteousness, and will hold thine hand, and will keep thee." Frankly, living a righteous life on planet Earth can often be hard. However, the Lord didn't call you just to turn around and abandon you. He will hold your hand and keep you upright. He will help you along the way.

Think of a baby boy just learning to walk. The baby's father holds his son's tiny hands and helps him take the first steps. That's what God does for us as our Father.

The Lord declares, "The former things are come to pass, and new things do I declare." God is speaking new things into your life, and as you walk in righteousness, these new things will overtake you. Believe in him and receive the new things he wants to do in you and for you!

Lord, help me to know that you are holding my hand as I walk in righteousness. I will receive the new things you have planned for my life.

Isaiah 43:1–2

*But now thus saith the L*ORD *that created thee, O Jacob, and he that formed thee, O Israel, Fear not: for I have redeemed thee, I have called thee by thy name; thou art mine. When thou passest through the waters, I will be with thee; and through the rivers, they shall not overflow thee: when thou walkest through the fire, thou shalt not be burned; neither shall the flame kindle upon thee.*

I recently heard a testimony of someone being healed of cancer. They had been devastated by the doctor's diagnosis; however, they began quoting this scriptural passage over their life. After much prayer, they returned to the doctor and, after tests, they were told the cancer was completely gone!

You serve a God who cares for you. He formed you, redeemed you, and called you by name. You are his! And just as a father takes care of his child, the Lord will defend you against anything this world throws in your face or places in your pathway. I don't know what waters or fires you are passing through, but I'm sure it's tough. Life has a way of blindsiding you sometimes. But I do know this: the Lord will be with you.

God, you formed me and called me by name. Remind me in my greatest trials that I am yours and that you are with me at all times.

Isaiah 43:10–11
Ye are my witnesses, saith the LORD, and my servant whom I have chosen: that ye may know and believe me, and understand that I am he: before me there was no God formed, neither shall there be after me. I,

> *even I, am the LORD; and beside me there is no saviour.*

Again, the Lord declares that he has chosen us. What has he chosen us for? So that we may know him. And the most fundamental thing we must know about him is that he is the one and only God. Before him there was no other god formed, and neither will there be after him. Beside him, there is no Savior.

We find in the New Testament that our Savior is Jesus. This does not contradict Isaiah's prophecy in Isaiah 43:10–11 because Jesus was the mighty God manifested in flesh, the revelation of God to humanity. Jesus was God's "express image" (Col. 1:15; Heb. 1:3). Jesus is the same God who was the Word in the beginning: "In the beginning was the Word and the Word was with God and the Word was God" (John 1:1). Jesus is the Lord, and beside him there is no Savior.

Jesus, you are my God and my Savior. You have chosen me. You existed before all else, and there is no god beside you—no one equal to you; no one who

can compare with you or compete with you. You and you alone are God.

Isaiah 43:18–19
Remember ye not the former things, neither consider the things of old. Behold, I will do a new thing; now it shall spring forth; shall ye not know it? I will even make a way in the wilderness, and rivers in the desert.

If you are in a desert place and feel it is time to come out, prophesy this verse over your life. God will do a new thing! He will make a way in the desert, and you will find it. Pray this verse prophetically.

Lord, I speak Isaiah's prophecy over my life. Do the new thing that you have for me and make a way through my wilderness. I will not be troubled by things in my past; I will look forward to the new things that are going to spring forth!

Isaiah 44:3–4
For I will pour water upon him that is thirsty, and floods upon the dry ground: I will pour my spirit upon

thy seed, and my blessing upon thine offspring: and they shall spring up as among the grass, as willows by the water courses.

Although I am not very old and experienced, I have realized one thing about the kingdom of God: "If anyone is thirsty, Jesus said, 'Let Him come.'" God can use those who are hungry and thirsty for more of him.

God doesn't hunt only for those with fine pedigrees when looking for someone to use, neither does he look among the worst of the worst. God uses the hungry and thirsty.

If you are thirsty for the things of God, you will be used, because God pours out water (his Spirit) upon those who are thirsty. He will bless that seed in your life and it will spring forth with blessings. Pray that you will be thirsty for more of him.

Lord, if I don't have anything else to offer you, I pray that you will make me thirsty for you. I desire your kingdom, your ministry, your presence, and your blessings. I am hungry and thirsty for a deeper relationship with you, Lord. Do not pass me by. Bless

me and pour out your Spirit upon me. I want more of you.

Isaiah 44:6
Thus saith the Lord the King of Israel, and his redeemer the Lord of hosts; I am the first, and I am the last; and beside me there is no God.

God is adamant about the fact that he is one. He is a jealous God and wants our praise to go only to him. He said he would not share his glory with another.

Jehovah or Yahweh ("Lord" in the KJV) claimed to be the first and the last. (See also Isa. 41:4.) Jesus claimed to be the first and the last (Rev. 1:8; 21:16; 22:13). Jesus said he was the "root and the offspring of David" (Rev. 22:16), meaning Jesus is both David's Lord and his descendant (Isaiah 11:1–10; Mark 12:35–37, Luke 20:41–44; Rom. 15:12; Rev. 5:5). There is no god beside him: "Hear, O Israel: The Lord our God is one Lord" (Deut. 6:4). The name "Jesus" means "Yahweh saves" or "Yahweh is salvation." Jesus, our Savior, is the incarnation of the Old Testament Lord.

God, you are my Savior! Thank you for being born of a woman and fulfilling your divine purpose to offer yourself on the cross to be the propitiation (sacrifice) for the sins of humanity. I praise you for your compassion, your boundless love, and your excellent greatness! (See John 15:13; 1 John 2:2.)

Isaiah 47:13–14

Thou art wearied in the multitude of thy counsels. Let now the astrologers, the stargazers, the monthly prognosticators, stand up, and save thee from these things that shall come upon thee. Behold, they shall be as stubble; the fire shall burn them; they shall not deliver themselves from the power of the flame: there shall not be a coal to warm at, nor fire to sit before it.

Isaiah 47 is a prediction of the ruin of Babylon. God had used this pagan nation to punish his people, but their cruel treatment of Judah had been so extreme that God had no other choice but to bring calamity upon them. Isaiah mocked the Babylonians for their penchant for consulting magicians, sorcerers, and astrologers, none of whom would be able to ward off the future destruction of Babylon. Their divinations were useless, like stubble that would burn up in the fire.

Proverbs 11:14 tells us there is safety in the multitude of counselors. The key to reconciling the counselors of Proverbs 11 and the counselors in Isaiah 47, is the contrast between godly and ungodly counsel. No good will come out of seeking answers from other sources besides God.

We can pray an important prayer from this passage. While godly counselors are good, beware of allowing too many people outside the church to speak into your life. In our day, people speak into our life through media more often than in person. Every google search, blog post, social media reel, or TV show is speaking into your life. Don't let the counsel that will be as stubble guide your future. Trust in the Lord, his word, and beware of these counselors.

Lord, help me to beware of people and media speaking into my life that are not of you. I want to listen to your counselors, not the counselors of this world.

Isaiah 49:8

Thus saith the LORD, In an acceptable time have I heard thee, and in a day of salvation have I helped thee: and I will preserve thee, and give thee for a covenant of the people, to establish the earth, to cause to inherit the desolate heritages.

The setting of this verse is a "Servant Song" promising that God's favor was once again turning to the exiles in Babylon, and they were at the point of covenant renewal. "The renewal of the covenant [found] expression in God's redemption, protection, provision, and guidance" (*Evangelical Commentary on the Bible*).

If you have strayed from the Lord, if you have been going through a time of chastisement or suffering through a trial, do not fear. No matter your situation, the Lord has not forgotten you. He will hear you in an "acceptable time" and turn to you with favor. Paul alluded to this promise in 2 Corinthians 6:2 (NIV): "For he says, 'In the time of my favor I heard you, and in the day of salvation I helped you.' I tell you, now is the time of God's favor, now is the day of salvation."

There is a day of salvation for you. Not only the day you receive salvation for your soul, but a day when God will bring you out of your situation. Continue to trust in him.

Lord, I pray that this will be the day of your favor in my life. I need your redemption, protection, provision, and guidance. Help me, Lord. You are my hope.

Isaiah 49:14–15
But Zion said, The LORD hath forsaken me, and my Lord hath forgotten me. Can a woman forget her sucking child, that she should not have compassion on the son of her womb? yea, they may forget, yet will I not forget thee.

The imagery in this verse is astounding. The exiled people of God were crying out, saying the Lord had forgotten them. The Lord responded, "Can a mother forget her nursing child? Can she feel no love for the child she has borne?" (NLT). God painted this picture of mother love as a comparison of his love for us. Then the Lord said, "But even if that were possible, I would not forget you!" (NLT).

We too often cry out that we feel the Lord has forgotten us. In times like these, think of the instinctive love and protection a mother has for her child and how she will fight for that child no matter what. But here is the beautiful thing: even if you are reading this book and your mother and father have abandoned you, you serve a God that will never leave you. He will never forget you. He loves you.

Lord, I pray that when I feel as though you've forgotten me, please remind me of this verse. Help me to remember that you love me and that what I am going through is part of your plan for my life.

Isaiah 50:4–11

The Lord God hath given me the tongue of the learned, that I should know how to speak a word in season to him that is weary: he wakeneth morning by morning, he wakeneth mine ear to hear as the learned. The Lord God hath opened mine ear, and I was not rebellious, neither turned away back. I gave my back to the smiters, and my cheeks to them that plucked off the hair: I hid not my face from shame and spitting. For the Lord God will help me; therefore shall I not be confounded: therefore have I set my face like a flint, and I know that I shall not be ashamed. He is near that justifieth me; who will contend with me? let us stand together: who is mine adversary? let him come near to me. Behold, the Lord God will help me; who is he that shall condemn me? lo, they all shall wax old as a garment; the moth shall eat them up. Who is among you that feareth the Lord, that obeyeth the voice of his servant, that walketh in darkness, and hath no light? let him trust in the name of the Lord, and stay upon his God. Behold, all ye that kindle a fire, that compass yourselves about with sparks: walk in the light of your fire, and in the sparks that ye have kindled. This shall ye have of mine hand; ye shall lie down in sorrow.

Isaiah 50 helped me through a very rough time. I pray it will help you through a season of hurt as well.

Verse 4 begins, "The Sovereign Lord has given me his words of wisdom, so that I know how to comfort the weary" (NLT). I've talked with many people who have made it through hard trials and discovered they are able to comfort and counsel others who are experiencing similar situations. It is the greatest joy to be able to comfort others!

Walking through a tough trial causes you to understand the fellowship of suffering. Others may be experiencing worlds of hurt, and because you have walked through a similar season of hurt, you will be able to be there for them. God will give you words of wisdom so you can speak into their life.

However, in order to do this, you must come forth as gold from your trial. Even if others hurt you, don't retaliate. You may experience shame, gossip, backstabbing, ridicule, and more. And the worst scenario is when those who come against you are in the church. Human nature wants to retaliate and rebel, whether it's against the church or the pastor—or God himself. But Isaiah wrote prophetically, speaking of the passion of Jesus before his death, "I was not rebellious."

After Isaiah painted this picture of the Suffering Servant enduring mockery, ridicule, and contempt, he continued, "For the Lord GOD will help me; therefore shall I not be confounded." Those first seven words have brought life to me in the darkest of times. When you cannot help yourself, God will help you!

Isaiah added that you will not be confounded. One of the hardest parts about going through a trial is wondering why it is happening: Why is God punishing me? What did I do wrong? Can I truly trust people—or even God?

I love what happened next: the Suffering Servant set his face like a flint. Flint is "a hard dark quartz that produces a spark when struck by steel" (www.merriam-webster.com). This conveys the idea that the Servant fixed his eyes on the glorious future ahead of him rather than the deep darkness he was going through. He was determined that he would obey, fulfill his mission, and refuse to be ashamed. The beating and spitting and mocking just seemed to bounce off because his face was set like a flint.

The final verse of this chapter says, "Behold, all ye that kindle a fire, that compass yourselves about with sparks: walk in the light of your fire, and in the sparks that ye have kindled." A flint is a rock that starts a fire. In ministry, we have to set our face and be determined to accomplish our mission. We can use our flint and our own fire for God to set other people on fire.

The youth pastor is kindling a fire among the young people. The worship leader is kindling a fire among the people who are singing and praising the Lord. The Bible study teacher is kindling a fire in people who have never heard the gospel. The missionary is kindling a fire in people of foreign lands. Every word of encouragement, every prayer you pray, and every time you comfort the broken, you are kindling a fire. You are sparking revival.

Isaiah said to walk by the light of the fire we are building. This was revelatory to me. We think we know the right thing to do for others. We think we can stir up a fire in others when they are down. But when life's hardest tests come our way, we ourselves can become discouraged or confounded.

But the Bible says to walk by the light of your own fire. All the prayers you've prayed for others— receive them for yourself. All the advice you've given to others—give it to yourself. All the serving and encouraging and comforting you've given to others—do it to yourself. The fire that you've stirred up for others can light your way as well.

Lord, I pray that through my trials you will teach me how to help others who are walking through similar circumstances. Give me a word in due season so that I may comfort them.

And Lord, even though it feels like people are doing me harm, I will not retaliate. Teach me that though I feel lost and don't understand, you will not leave me confounded. Through it all, you will help me. I will set my face like a flint, just as you did before your greatest trial. I will look forward to the good you have planned for my future. I will be a spark of revival not only for myself but for others. In Jesus' name.

Isaiah 52:12
For ye shall not go out with haste, nor go by flight: for the LORD will go before you; and the God of Israel will be your rereward.

The Jews were exiled in Babylon for seventy years. A few were old enough to remember the horror of their capture and deportation. Thousands had been born in Babylon since then and therefore were reluctant to leave the only home they had ever known. But in chapter 52, Isaiah, speaking prophetically, indicated their exodus from Babylon would be far different than their exodus from Egypt. Israelites had fled their Egyptian taskmasters in great haste, hotly pursued by Pharaoh's army. Now, through Isaiah, the Lord promised their exodus from Babylon would not be a desperate flight; it would be a triumphant march.

Someone reading this verse for the first time might think the word "rereward" is just an old-fashioned spelling of "reward." That is not the case, however. "Rereward" is a Middle English word from Anglo-French: *arere* (behind) and *gard* (guard). In King James English it meant "the troops in the rear of an army on the march." In other words, the rereward protected the army from behind. In Joshua 6:9, as God's people were about to take Jericho, God's marching order was (1) the warriors, (2) the priests blowing their trumpets, (3) the ark, and (4) the rear guard. *Rereward* is no longer used in the English language, but understanding its original usage brings new meaning to Isaiah 52:12.

There is power for you in this prophecy. God goes before you in your battles, trials, and decisions. Not only has he prepared the way before you, but you don't have to worry about your past sneaking up from behind—because God has your back.

God, thank you for not only going before me, but for protecting me from my past. And thank you for giving me power to fight my battles. I can be victorious when you are at my side.

Isaiah 53:5
But he was wounded for our transgressions, he was bruised for our iniquities: the chastisement of our peace was upon him; and with his stripes we are healed.

Isaiah 53 is a prophecy of Jesus Christ. His story of the cross is written throughout the chapter. Verse 5 is one of the clear indicators of this parallel: Jesus was wounded, bruised, and beaten at Calvary. He was chastised by the guards and railed upon by the crowd. The stripes he took on his back were for our healing. Several New Testament writers referenced this chapter (Matt. 8:17; John 12:38; Acts 8:29–39; Rom. 10:16). In this prayer, we thank Jesus for what he did on the cross.

Jesus, thank you for laying your life down on the cross and taking my sins upon you. Thank you for submitting to the stripes, the mockers, the thorns, the nails, and death. You took the bruises and stripes for my healing. Thank you, Lord, for enduring the cross that I might experience your salvation, comfort, and peace that passes all understanding.

Isaiah 54:4

Fear not; for thou shalt not be ashamed: neither be thou confounded; for thou shalt not be put to shame: for thou shalt forget the shame of thy youth, and shalt not remember the reproach of thy widowhood any more.

If you didn't grow up with the best home life, you can speak this prayer. God is for you. You do not have to be ashamed or confounded. If you know the Lord, you can forget the shame of your youth and whatever that entails. This is a beautiful prayer of redemption. Speak it!

God, I pray that I would not be ashamed or confounded about my upbringing. Cause me to forget the shame, fear, mistreatment, or hurt. You are my loving Father, Jesus.

Isaiah 54:17
No weapon that is formed against thee shall prosper; and every tongue that shall rise against thee in judgment thou shalt condemn. This is the heritage of the servants of the LORD, and their righteousness is of me, saith the LORD.

I didn't hit my growth spurt until I was in my late teens, therefore I was a pretty small kid. When I entered high school, I was still a short kid that weighed less than a hundred pounds. And while I never got physically bullied, I probably would have been a pushover for anyone who wanted to.

I'll never forget one summer camp where there were all sorts of pranks, bullying, and messing with people's belongings going on. It seemed like nobody was safe. But I had a friend at the camp who was older than I. He was known as a troublemaker, but he came to me and said, "Hey, don't worry. I got your back. Nobody is going to mess with your stuff."

While my troublemaker friend certainly wasn't like God, I thought of him when I read this verse. Why? Because God is basically saying, "Nobody is going to mess with you. I got your back. You are my heritage, and I will protect you." The NLT says, "No weapon turned against you will succeed." No physical action. No threats or cursing. No darts from the enemy. No plots to do you in. Nothing. Because you are part of his family. And God protects his kids.

God, thank you for the benefits I have as one of your heirs. Thank you for protecting me. I choose to live in your heritage. You are my Lord, my God, and my Father. Amen.

Isaiah 55:8–9

For my thoughts are not your thoughts, neither are your ways my ways, saith the LORD. For as the heavens are higher than the earth, so are my ways higher than your ways, and my thoughts than your thoughts.

I remind myself of this verse quite often. The Lord's thoughts are better than mine. His vantage point allows him to see the big picture, the grand scheme, the outcome of my days. We really should trust him more than we trust ourselves because his ways are higher than the heavens. His thoughts are higher than our thoughts!

Trusting in his thoughts means submitting fully to him, living a life worthy of your calling, and walking in the Spirit. Beyond that, don't worry. You may not be able to see past the end of your nose, but God can see far into the future. To you, it may look like something is going to end in disaster, but he knows the end from the beginning. He has it all thought out. He knows the way you should take, so follow his lead, and then don't worry.

Lord, I submit to your thoughts and your ways for my life. I choose not to worry when life doesn't seem to go right in my eyes. I will trust you to lead me in the right way.

Isaiah 56:1–5

Thus saith the LORD, Keep ye judgment, and do justice: for my salvation is near to come, and my righteousness to be revealed. Blessed is the man that doeth this, and the son of man that layeth hold on it; that keepeth the sabbath from polluting it, and keepeth his hand from doing any evil. Neither let the son of the stranger, that hath joined himself to the LORD, speak, saying, The LORD hath utterly separated me from his people: neither let the eunuch say, Behold, I am a dry tree. For thus saith the LORD unto the eunuchs that keep my sabbaths, and choose the things that please me, and take hold of my covenant; even unto them will I give in mine house and within my walls a place and a name better than of sons and of daughters: I will give them an everlasting name, that shall not be cut off.

This declaration from God is one of my favorite portions of Isaiah, and it ties to one of my favorite stories in the New Testament. But first I must dip back into the Old Testament to give this story a foundation. Deuteronomy 23:1 (NIV) says, "No one who has been emasculated by crushing or cutting may enter the assembly of the LORD." This law was referring to eunuchs, who were not allowed to participate in the religious rites of the people of God.

In Acts 8, Philip was in the middle of a red-hot revival in Samaria when the Spirit of the Lord interrupted and told him he was needed on the Desert Road that led to Gaza. Philip obeyed, and finally came upon a man riding in a chariot, who was a eunuch.

Eunuchs cannot father children; therefore, they have no one to carry on the family name and no heirs to receive a legacy. In pagan societies, eunuchs were often placed in charge of harems, but that wasn't this Ethiopian eunuch's position; he was the treasurer in charge of the riches of Candace, queen of Ethiopia!

This eunuch would have been known as a God-fearer because he had been to Jerusalem to worship, although he hadn't been allowed to participate in the religious rites of the Jews.

When Philip "joined himself" to the chariot, he heard the eunuch reading Isaiah's prophecy concerning Jesus (Isa. 53.) The Lord had noticed this eunuch because he had "joined himself to the LORD" (Isa. 56:3) despite the physical condition that, up to now, had denied him a place in God's house. In essence, the Lord was saying to the eunuch, "I will give you a place and a name better than sons and daughters." (See Isa. 56:3–5.) Using these passages in Isaiah, Philip preached about Jesus' death, burial, and resurrection. He told the eunuch that he indeed had a place in the assembly of God's people if he would obey Acts 2:38, the same message Peter had preached on the Day of Pentecost.

As they rode along, they came to some water, and, full of faith and bolstered by the encouragement of Philip's words, the eunuch said excitedly, "Look, here is water. What can stand in the way of my being baptized?" (Acts 8:36, NIV). They both went down into the water and Philip baptized the eunuch. That is the first prayer we can derive from Isaiah 53 and 56.

The second prayer is for those who love God but still feel as if they have nothing—no heritage or legacy, no family or godly home—yet they continue to walk down the road to relationship. "The Sovereign LORD, who brings back the outcasts of Israel, says: 'I will bring others, too, besides my people Israel'" (Isa. 56:8, NLT). God has a place and a name and a family for you! You too can pray these passages.

God, I want to be baptized in your name so I can enter your assembly. Thank you for giving me a place in your family and making me a joint heir with you. (See Rom. 8:14–17.)

Isaiah 56:7
Even them will I bring to my holy mountain, and make them joyful in my house of prayer: their burnt offerings and their sacrifices shall be accepted upon mine altar; for mine house shall be called an house of prayer for all people.

I want my body in which the Holy Spirit dwells to be a house of prayer. I want my home to be a house of prayer. I want my church to be a house of prayer. I want to be known as a person who prays.

Lord, make me a house of prayer.

Isaiah 58:5–12

Is it such a fast that I have chosen? a day for a man to afflict his soul? is it to bow down his head as a bulrush, and to spread sackcloth and ashes under him? wilt thou call this a fast, and an acceptable day to the Lord? Is not this the fast that I have chosen? to loose the bands of wickedness, to undo the heavy burdens, and to let the oppressed go free, and that ye break every yoke? Is it not to deal thy bread to the hungry, and that thou bring the poor that are cast out to thy house? when thou seest the naked, that thou cover him; and that thou hide not thyself from thine own flesh? Then shall thy light break forth as the morning, and thine health shall spring forth speedily: and thy righteousness shall go before thee; the glory of the Lord shall be thy rereward. Then shalt thou call, and the Lord shall answer; thou shalt cry, and he shall say, Here I am. If thou take away from the midst of thee the yoke, the putting forth of the finger, and speaking vanity; and if thou draw out thy soul to the hungry, and satisfy the afflicted soul; then shall thy light rise in obscurity, and thy darkness be as the noon day: and the LORD shall guide thee continually, and satisfy thy soul in drought, and make fat thy bones: and thou shalt be like a watered garden, and like a spring of water, whose waters fail not. And they that shall be of thee shall build the old waste places: thou shalt raise up the foundations of many generations; and thou shalt be called, The repairer of the breach, The restorer of paths to dwell in.

Isaiah 58 discloses the type of fast that pleases God. Your fasting will be of great benefit if you will read, pray, and obey Isaiah 58.

First, the Lord says in verse 3 that we should not fast to please ourselves. The NLT says, "'We have fasted before you,' they say. 'Why aren't you impressed? We have been very hard on ourselves, and you don't even notice it!' 'I will tell you why,' I respond. 'It's because you are fasting to please yourselves.'" The Pharisees were good at this. One Pharisee even went to the temple and boasted, "God, I thank you that I'm not like other men . . . I fast twice a week!" God described fasts like these as hypocritical. People who fast to please themselves "try to look miserable and disheveled so people [will] admire them in their fast" (Matt. 6:16, NLT).

Fasting is a waste of time if, on an empty stomach, you sate your mind with ungodly media. Furthermore, a rumbling stomach tends to make one a little testy, so the Lord warns you not to fight with others. Fasting is not an excuse to be grouchy.

Instead, fasting is a time to humble yourself before God and surrender to him. When you do this, verse 6 says God will do amazing things in you and for you and through you: (1) loose the bands of wickedness, (2) undo heavy burdens, (3) let the oppressed go free, and (4) break every bondage of sin.

Verse 7 says to give to the poor during a fast. Reading this verse at one point convicted me, so I decided that when I went on a fast, I would take the money I would have spent on food and give grocery store gift cards to strangers. They may not be poor in a literal sense, but they are poor in spirit. Another idea would be to ask your pastor if he knows anyone in the church or in the community who needs assistance. You never know how far an act of kindness will go in the kingdom of God.

Next, "Thy light shall break forth as the morning, and thine health shall spring forth speedily." Fasting will bring you out of your darkest trial and bring health to your body. It works. I have experienced it, and I know others who have experienced it as well.

Isaiah continued, "The glory of the Lord shall be thy rereward." (Refer to the discussion of the word "rereward" in Isaiah 52:12.) This is another great benefit you will incur from extended fasting. The NLT says, "Your salvation will come like the dawn, and your wounds will heal quickly. Your godliness will lead you forward, and the glory of the Lord will protect you from behind." God will be your rear guard.

The chapter concludes by saying the Lord will give you light in your obscurity, guide you continually, satisfy your soul during dry times, add blessings to your life, "reestablish the ancient foundations" (NET) of your life, and restore your paths.

Fasting works. It is powerful, but it is not easy. Your flesh does not want to fast. Pray that God will lead you to an extended fast and that he will give you the strength, knowledge, wisdom, and the right time to fast.

God, I want to experience all you have for me through fasting. And as I'm on my fast, I will pray this chapter over my life. In Jesus' name.

Isaiah 59:1
Behold, the Lord's hand is not shortened, that it cannot save; neither his ear heavy, that it cannot hear.

Different prayers in Scripture will click with different people. For instance, when I first began praying the word, I started with Psalm 23. Isaiah 59:1 also had special meaning for me not because I prayed it often, but because I heard it prayed often by one of my youth pastors. I remember hearing it at youth prayer, on Sunday, at youth services, and more. This verse obviously spoke volumes into my youth pastor's life. I still remember his voice crying out, "Your arm is not too short that it cannot save! Your ear is not too heavy that it cannot hear!"

Let the word of God speak to you. As you read through the Scriptures searching for prayers to pray, allow the Spirit to direct you. Some of those passages will become a part of you and your normal prayer time.

Lord, you can reach into my innermost being. You hear my every cry and every word I pray. Your powerful arm can reach all who need you, no matter how deep they are in sin. Reach for _____ today. Hear their cry and heal, rescue, and save them, I pray. In Jesus' name!

Isaiah 59:16

And he saw that there was no man, and wondered that there was no intercessor: therefore his arm brought salvation unto him; and his righteousness, it sustained him.

An intercessor is someone who stands in the gap for another. The greatest example of an intercessor is

Jesus Christ. We deserved to receive punishment for our own sin, but Jesus willingly took our sins upon himself. He submitted to the scourge, felt the agony of the nails, shed his precious blood, and died on a cross for us.

We also can be intercessors. Leonard Ravenhill said, "The most selfless person in the world is an intercessor." True intercessors are kind of rare in the church for several reasons: (1) intercessors must submit their time to the Lord because the spirit of intercession could come upon them at any moment; (2) intercessors may never know the results of their prayers or even the people they are praying for; (3) intercessors may experience deep pain and groaning in their spirit without understanding the reason behind the prayer. But the intercessor is the most powerful (and probably the most unknown or unacknowledged) member of your church.

Isaiah said the Lord searched for an intercessor. This should bring conviction to our hearts. The role of the intercessor is the most selfless yet often the most needed ministry within the church. Who is willing to fall on their face in private and weep for the lost souls of the world? Who will groan and cry that the Lord will reunite the broken family, be a father to the orphan, feed the hungry, comfort the mistreated, and set the captive free? Who will agonize over the soul that is searching for the source of all life? Lord, make us intercessors.

Lord, I pray that you will make me an intercessor. I am making myself available to you at all times, day or night. Don't let me be so busy with my plans that I cannot kneel and cry out in prayer when you say to intercede. I want to be an intercessor.

Isaiah 59:19
So shall they fear the name of the LORD from the west, and his glory from the rising of the sun. When the enemy shall come in like a flood, the Spirit of the LORD shall lift up a standard against him.

In battle, the standard-bearer was a person toward the front of the charge that carried the standard or flag. The standard gave the soldier a visual signal of where his unit was; therefore, the loss of a standard was considered one of the worst things that could happen in a battle.

The Lord is our standard-bearer. He died and rose again to live forever, assuring us we will never lose our standard-bearer. When the enemy comes in like a flood, we don't have to worry about defeat because the Lord is leading the charge. And no enemy can ever stand against his battle strategy, his might, his powerful weapons, or his strong right arm.

When we feel the attack of the enemy, we can speak this prayer over our life.

When the enemy comes in like a flood, your Spirit will raise up a standard against him. Just as surely as you protected the Israelites when they were crossing the Jordan River in flood stage, you are my protection from the floods the enemy sends my way.

Isaiah 60:1–2

Arise, shine; for thy light is come, and the glory of the LORD is risen upon thee. For, behold, the darkness shall cover the earth, and gross darkness the people:

but the Lord shall arise upon thee, and his glory shall be seen upon thee.

It may seem as though you're surrounded by darkness, but it's time to get up! The light of God's glory is shining!

Lord, although I'm walking in darkness, I pray for your light. Let your glory and light shine down upon me.

Isaiah 61:1–3
The Spirit of the Lord God is upon me; because the Lord hath anointed me to preach good tidings unto the meek; he hath sent me to bind up the brokenhearted, to proclaim liberty to the captives, and the opening of the prison to them that are bound; to proclaim the acceptable year of the Lord, and the day of vengeance of our God; to comfort all that mourn; to appoint unto them that mourn in Zion, to give unto them beauty for ashes, the oil of joy for mourning, the garment of praise for the spirit of heaviness; that they might be called trees of

righteousness, the planting of the LORD, that he might be glorified.

Many will recognize this passage. Jesus, after his forty-day fast and temptation, returned to Galilee, teaching in the synagogues. When he came to Nazareth, his hometown, he was invited to read from the Scripture, and he chose this passage in Isaiah. (See Luke 4:14–20.) He concluded by saying, "This day is this scripture fulfilled in your ears" (Luke 4:21).

I believe we should pray this passage over our own life. We should pray that the Spirit of the Lord will be upon us to enable us to preach boldness to the meek, bind up the wounds of the brokenhearted, proclaim liberty to the captives and deliverance to the bound, to offer beauty for ashes, the oil of joy for mourning, and the garment of praise for the spirit of heaviness, and to proclaim the acceptable year of the Lord.

Prophesy this word to your friends. Your encouraging word in a broken situation is led by the Spirit of the Lord. Your preaching (telling forth) of good things is "anointed prophecy." Speak life.

Lord, I will speak life to the broken, captive, bound, and mourning. Let your Spirit be upon me to speak and preach your word. You are coming soon, and I will proclaim it.

Isaiah 64:4
For since the beginning of the world men have not heard, nor perceived by the ear, neither hath the eye seen, O God, beside thee, what he hath prepared for him that waiteth for him.

God has greater things prepared for us than we could ever imagine, both here on Earth and up in Heaven. I want the things God has prepared for me.

God, I will wait on the things you have prepared for me. Give me patience to wait on you. Your plans are greater than I could ever imagine.

Isaiah 65:24
And it shall come to pass, that before they call, I will answer; and while they are yet speaking, I will hear.

This verse is powerful! God is omniscient, meaning he possesses universal or complete knowledge. He can see you even before you feel a need to pray. He already has the answer waiting, but you must still pray and believe that while you are still speaking, God is working on your behalf.

God, I believe that even as I am praying to you, you have already heard my cry and are about to do what only you can do. Help me to understand the power in my prayers.

JEREMIAH

Jeremiah 1:5

Before I formed thee in the belly I knew thee; and before thou camest forth out of the womb I sanctified thee, and I ordained thee a prophet unto the nations.

The book of Jeremiah begins with a personal word from the Lord to this prophet, stating that before Jeremiah was born, God had sanctified him and called him to be a prophet unto the nations.

Your calling is not the same as Jeremiah's, but know this: God had a plan, a purpose, and a calling for you before you were born. And you need to walk in that calling.

Lord, you had a plan for me even as you were forming me in my mother's womb. I will walk in this calling according to your will. You are amazing!

Jeremiah 1:9–10

Then the LORD put forth his hand, and touched my mouth. And the LORD said unto me, Behold, I have put my words in thy mouth. See, I have this day set thee over the nations and over the kingdoms, to root out, and to pull down, and to destroy, and to throw down, to build, and to plant.

As you start walking by faith in your calling, you will have questions. What do I do? What do I say? Where should I go? When should I start? Whom should I listen to? These questions are valid.

The Lord responded to Jeremiah by saying, "I will put the words in your mouth." God will give you the words to speak. But take note of this next part: "I have set you over nations and kingdoms." Jeremiah did not promote himself; God placed him in that position. Then God told Jeremiah what he was supposed to do: "I have set you to root out, pull down, destroy, build, and plant." The Lord will teach you what you are supposed to do.

I was only seventeen when I first started preaching, and I found it difficult to discover what my role as a preacher should be. My journey of discovery was much too involved to write about in this book because the nature of my ministry seemed to keep changing depending on my location.

However, I had one transformative conversation with God that I will always remember. I learned that he wants me to speak life wherever I go. As my ministry progressed, I received much more instruction, experience, and learning, but that memorable conversation gave me clear understanding that my mission was to speak life.

Ask God to reveal what he wants you to do in ministry. He won't give you all the pieces to the puzzle at once, but you will receive principles that will stay with you all of your life.

Lord, as I begin to walk in my calling, I pray you will give me the words to speak, tell me what to do, and provide principles to guide me everywhere I go. I will continually pray for these things.

Jeremiah 3:12–15

Go and proclaim these words toward the north, and say, Return, thou backsliding Israel, saith the LORD; and I will not cause mine anger to fall upon you: for I am merciful, saith the LORD, and I will not keep anger for ever. Only acknowledge thine iniquity, that thou hast transgressed against the LORD thy God, and hast scattered thy ways to the strangers under every green tree, and ye have not obeyed my voice, saith the LORD. Turn, O backsliding children, saith the LORD; for I am married unto you: and I will take you one of a city, and two of a family, and I will bring you to Zion: and I will give you pastors according to mine heart, which shall feed you with knowledge and understanding.

When you sin, your response should be to ask God for forgiveness and then renew your relationship with him. He wants you back! He will not stay angry very long. He loves you with an everlasting love. Come back to him!

Once your relationship with God is reestablished, one of the most important people in your life will be your pastor. He is God's gift to you. (See Eph. 4:8, 11.) The Lord says, "I will give you shepherds after my own heart, who will lead you with knowledge and understanding." This is a beautiful picture of the church. Pray over your life and for your pastor.

Lord, I repent of every sin I've committed against you. I will return to you, trusting in your love. And I pray for my pastor, who loves me as you do and who teaches me with knowledge and understanding. I will submit to my pastor, as he loves me and cares for my soul.

Jeremiah 5:4–5
Therefore I said, Surely these are poor; they are foolish: for they know not the way of the LORD, nor the judgment of their God. I will get me unto the great men, and will speak unto them; for they have known the way of the LORD, and the judgment of their God: but these have altogether broken the yoke, and burst the bonds.

There is no counsel like godly counsel. There is no advice like godly advice. Be sure to find "great men" from which to seek advice.

What is the mark of a great man or woman? "They have known the way of the Lord, and the judgment of their God." Pray for access to godly counsel in your life.

Lord, when making a tough decision I want to seek counsel of godly men and women. When I'm not sure where to go, what to do, or how to fix the problems around me, I will seek advice from people who have the mind of Christ.

Jeremiah 6:16–17
Thus saith the Lord, Stand ye in the ways, and see, and ask for the old paths, where is the good way, and walk therein, and ye shall find rest for your souls. But they said, We will not walk therein. Also I set watchmen over you, saying, Hearken to the sound of the trumpet. But they said, We will not hearken.

Jeremiah was very young when God called him. His ministry began about seventy-five years after Isaiah's ministry during the reign of King Josiah and extended possibly twenty years after the deportation from

Jerusalem. King Josiah was instrumental in generating one of the greatest revivals in Judah's history (2 Kings 22–23).

However, the good things Josiah had wrought in Judah didn't last long, as after his death he was succeeded by four wicked kings. Jeremiah's preaching included indictments of the people's turning against God, their injustices, their false words, and their false leaders. His "messages always placed him at odds with the people, particularly the religious and political leadership of Judah in the time leading up to and immediately following the destruction of Jerusalem" (Apostolic Study Bible).

Although the Jews did not appreciate it, Jeremiah was God's gift to them. If they had heeded Jeremiah's messages and turned to the Lord, God would have accepted them. Jeremiah preached, "Stand at the crossroads and look; ask for the ancient paths, ask where the good way is, and walk in it" (v. 16, NIV).

When we find ourselves straying from the truth of the word, we should look back to what our elders did. Tradition is not always biblically based, but it usually was established for a good reason. As T. F. Tenney used to say, "Before you move a fence you need to find out who put it there and why they built it." Look back at the good paths and walk in them!

The Lord said he would appoint watchmen over us—our pastor and the godly leaders in our life. Heed what they have to say; it will spare you a lot of grief. The Israelites wouldn't obey Jeremiah's words and suffered the consequences. We are wise when we submit to our leaders. Only then will our souls find rest.

God, I will not stray from the good old paths that you have established. I will follow the leading of my pastor and the godly leaders in my life. And I pray that my soul will find rest in you.

Jeremiah 9:23–24
Thus saith the LORD, Let not the wise man glory in his wisdom, neither let the mighty man glory in his might, let not the rich man glory in his riches: but let him that glorieth glory in this, that he understandeth and knoweth me, that I am the LORD which exercise

lovingkindness, judgment, and righteousness, in the earth: for in these things I delight, saith the LORD.

What does it mean to glory in something? To think it's great? To be proud? To boast? Glorying in something means you are lifting that thing up above other things in your life. God said in Isaiah 42:8 that he will not give his glory to another. Paul referenced Jeremiah 9:23–24 in 1 Corinthians 1:29–31: "That no flesh should glory in his presence. But of him are ye in Christ Jesus, who of God is made unto us wisdom, and righteousness, and sanctification, and redemption: that, according as it is written, He that glorieth, let him glory in the Lord."

That is why we glorify God and him alone. It is good to glory in understanding the word and knowing the Lord.

Lord, I will glory in you alone. I thank you for your lovingkindness, your judgment, and your righteousness. I lift you up above all other things in my life.

Jeremiah 13:15

Hear ye, and give ear; be not proud: for the LORD hath spoken.

Pride is a killer. Proverbs 16:18 says, "Pride goeth before destruction, and an haughty spirit before a fall." We must constantly guard against pride in our lives—not the pride, for instance, that one feels after a job well done or in a friend or relative's accomplishments, but the kind of pride that "stems from self-righteousness or conceit." God hates that kind of pride not only because it is sinful, but because it hinders one from seeking him.

Pride can be described in two ways. First, the pride that boasts loudly, "I am the best!" The Lord has given you talents and abilities, but don't pride yourself when excelling in them. Keep this pride in check because it leads to not wanting or needing anyone, even God.

Second, the pride that moans, "I am nothing and will never amount to anything." Yes, this also is pride, and it is depressing and demeaning. It leads to not trusting anyone and not doing anything for the kingdom. The Lord has a purpose for you, he has called you, and he has equipped you, so who are you to say you are not able?

God, I pray against pride in my life. Help me to humble myself before you. I need you in all areas of my life. I pray that I would be confident, yet humble.

Jeremiah 17:7–10
Blessed is the man that trusteth in the LORD, and whose hope the LORD is. For he shall be as a tree planted by the waters, and that spreadeth out her roots by the river, and shall not see when heat cometh, but her leaf shall be green; and shall not be careful in the year of drought, neither shall cease from yielding fruit. The heart is deceitful above all things, and desperately wicked: who can know it? I the LORD search the heart, I try the reins, even to give every man according to his ways, and according to the fruit of his doings.

When you trust in God, your environment and circumstances don't matter. He will take care of you.

Even if it feels like you're in a desert or suffering through a drought, God will maintain your health in that unhealthy environment in the areas you need, whether physical, emotional, spiritual, or mental.

Don't trust in your feelings. Your heart is a deceitful seedbed of wickedness. You won't always feel like doing, saying, listening to, or watching the right things, but if you truly trust God, you'll do the right thing. So be aware that your feelings can and will lie. Trust the Lord and his word.

Lord, I will trust you with my doings. Even when my environment doesn't look like it could possibly promote growth, I pray that you will take care of me and help me to do the right thing and grow in you.

Jeremiah 18:1–4

The word which came to Jeremiah from the LORD, saying, Arise, and go down to the potter's house, and there I will cause thee to hear my words. Then I went down to the potter's house, and, behold, he wrought a work on the wheels. And the vessel that he made of clay was marred in the hand of the potter: so he made it again another vessel, as seemed good to the potter to make it.

Your Creator formed your physical body, your characteristics, and your traits while you were in the womb. But that was only the beginning. If you will allow him to, he will continue to work on you throughout your lifetime until you are shaped in his own image (cf. Eph. 4:13).

The Lord gave Jeremiah an object lesson at the pottery. Jeremiah watched as the potter worked with the clay. The vessel looked like it was shaping up beautifully, but somehow the clay became marred in the process and the potter had to start over. As the wheel started turning, the potter kept adding water to keep the clay moist and malleable in his hands. When the vessel was finally finished, it was beautiful, stable, and secure. This is what the Lord is doing in your life. Isaiah 64:8 says, "O LORD, . . . we are the clay, and thou our potter; and we all are the work of thy hands."

Sometimes as the wheel is whirring and you're spinning around and being worked over, you might get the feeling you don't really like what is happening. You think, *Wait! I never wanted to be that kind of vessel!* You cry out, "Stop! You're doing it wrong! . . . How clumsy can you be?" (Isa. 45:9, NLT). But the prophet Isaiah warned against resisting the potter: "Doom to you who fight your Maker—you're a pot at odds with the potter!" (MSG). Paul wrote, "Does not the potter have the right to make out of the same lump of clay some pottery for special purposes and some for common use?" (Rom. 9:21, NIV).

Give the potter complete control over your life because he's the one who formed you in the womb, and he knows everything about you—even to the furthest reach of your potential. He wants to form you into a vessel that is suited to his purpose for your life.

Lord, shape me and mold me into what you want me to be. You are the potter and I am the clay. I will not resist the work you are doing in me. I am placing my life in your hands.

Jeremiah 20:9

Then I said, I will not make mention of him, nor speak any more in his name. But his word was in mine heart as a burning fire shut up in my bones, and I was weary with forbearing, and I could not stay.

Jeremiah was a powerful preacher, and his messages of impending doom riled everyone from the king to the priests to the nobles and down to the common people. No one wanted to hear the warning that if they didn't turn to the Lord their city was going to be destroyed and they were going to be attacked, killed, and the rest taken into captivity for their idolatry and sin.

One day Jeremiah went to Topheth, a place in the Hinnom Valley where Baal and Molech were worshiped and children were sacrificed. He preached a rip-snorting message about how God was going to break his people like a potter breaks a defective vessel and throws it in on the trash heap. The Lord was going to bring disaster on Jerusalem and the surrounding towns, and people would be slaughtered without mercy.

This so enraged Priest Pashur that his blood boiled. He ordered that Jeremiah be scourged and thrown overnight into a cell and his arms and legs put in stocks.

The next day, when Pashur released the prophet, Jeremiah spoke the same message to the priest, adding greater detail. He said the Lord had changed the priest's name to "The Man Who Lives in Terror." He predicted Pashur's capture and that he would be taken to Babylon where he would die. (See Jer. 20:3–6, NLT.)

Jeremiah must have sunk into depression after the adrenaline wore off, because he began complaining to the Lord. Everyone made fun of his rantings and ravings about violence and destruction to the extent he had become a household joke and people mocked him in the streets. He thought, *My life would be so much easier if I quit delivering the Lord's messages*. But this was impossible. Whenever he tried to keep quiet, the Lord's words became like a fire in his bones that he couldn't contain. He *had* to keep preaching!

Thankfully, our primary message to the world is one of salvation, not destruction. We should desire the word of God to be so strong in us that we must tell someone about it, even if some people mock us or reject our words. This desire should push us to give our testimony and proclaim the good news of the gospel message. It should be like a fire shut up in our bones.

God, let your word be like a fire shut up in my bones. I will speak it, pray it, and proclaim it!

Jeremiah 23:16
Thus saith the LORD of hosts, Hearken not unto the words of the prophets that prophesy unto you: they make you vain: they speak a vision of their own heart, and not out of the mouth of the LORD.

Pastor Matt Jones, in his blog "The Message and Ministry of the False Prophets in Jeremiah" (delreychurch.com) said Jeremiah was perceived as a "Chicken-Little who warned the people that the sky was truly falling." Jeremiah was mocked and persecuted because false prophets went everywhere contradicting everything he preached, telling the people they were safe and nothing was going to happen to them. The false prophets' words gave the people a false sense of security.

Jeremiah had much to say about these charlatans: "Do not listen to these prophets when they prophesy to you, filling you with futile hopes. They are making up everything they say. They do not speak for the Lord" (NLT).

False prophets abound in our day. Sometimes they're hard to recognize because they don't call themselves prophets. They will speak to you and over your life without you realizing it. They will speak a vision of their own making and influence you to turn your desires to their desires.

We can protect ourselves by following the advice of John: "Beloved, do not believe every spirit, but test every spirit to see if they are from God, for many false prophets have gone out into the world" (1 John 4:1, ESV). One of the tests is to determine whether that person's beliefs agree with God's word. Another way is to wait and see if the person's prediction comes to pass. If it doesn't, then that person didn't hear from the Lord; he made everything up.

Lord, make me aware of false prophets and people who speak the wrong vision into my heart and mind. I want to follow what you envision for me.

Jeremiah 29:7
And seek the peace of the city whither I have caused you to be carried away captives, and pray unto the LORD for it: for in the peace thereof shall ye have peace.

Jeremiah wrote a letter to the exiles in Babylon, urging them to "work for the peace and prosperity of the city where I sent you into exile. Pray to the Lord for it, for its welfare will determine your welfare" (NLT).

These captives were in a bad situation. Some might say they deserved it because, although they had been adequately warned, they had refused to listen to Jeremiah and other true prophets of his day. However, even in the exiles' hardship, God was still offering peace. Jeremiah told them in his letter that they would be in Babylon for seventy years, and afterward the Lord would bring them back home and do for them the good things he had promised. Then comes of oft-quoted verse: "For I know the plans I have for you, says the LORD. They are plans for good and not for disaster, to give you a future and a hope. In those days when you pray, I will listen" (Jer. 29:11, NLT).

You may be in a bad situation (possibly of your own making), but there is still opportunity for peace. There is still room for hope. God still has good plans for you. You won't be in that bad situation forever, and when you pray to the Lord, he will hear your prayer.

So seek the peace of God. For when you seek peace, God will grant it.

God, I will seek your peace even in my captivity of my own wrongdoing. And I pray that you will grant me peace, even though I don't deserve it.

Jeremiah 29:11–13
For I know the thoughts that I think toward you, saith the LORD, thoughts of peace, and not of evil, to give you an expected end. Then shall ye call upon me, and

ye shall go and pray unto me, and I will hearken unto you. And ye shall seek me, and find me, when ye shall search for me with all your heart.

The Bible says we are living in "evil days" (Eph. 5:25–16; 2 Tim. 3:1–8). In times like these, we need to read Jeremiah 29:11–13 over our lives.

Not sure why your life isn't working out? Don't worry. God has it all thought out. Not sure why you have to deal with _____? (Fill in the blank.) God has thoughts of peace for you, so just hold on. Pray to him, and he will hear you. Seek for him with all your heart, and you will find him. Don't ever doubt that God is for you. His plan is for you to be at peace, knowing he will give you an expected end—the good ending he has prepared for you. His plan for the rest of your life will be better than the beginning. So keep on searching after him because, through your search, he will reveal his plans for you.

Lord, thank you for the thoughts and plans you have for my life. Help me not to worry when evil seems to surround me. Your thoughts for me are peace, and so

I receive your peace. And through it all, I will search for you until I find you.

Jeremiah 30:2
Thus speaketh the Lord God of Israel, saying, Write thee all the words that I have spoken unto thee in a book.

Journaling should be an important part of your prayer life. When God speaks to you in prayer, through his word, or through someone else, write it down. Remember it. Continue to speak it. Let it encourage you in times of discouragement.

My phone notes are my journal, and I wouldn't be able to continue without them. One note contains every big moment that God spoke to me. Another is full of scriptural passages and words from the Lord. I turn to them when I feel discouraged or depressed. Still other notes recall various situations in my life.

We have the word of God today because holy men of old "wrote it down"—they wrote the Lord's message to mankind. Learn from this passage in

Jeremiah and write down whatever the Lord says to you.

God, when you speak, I will write it down.

Jeremiah 31:3–6

The LORD hath appeared of old unto me, saying, Yea, I have loved thee with an everlasting love: therefore with lovingkindness have I drawn thee. Again I will build thee, and thou shalt be built, O virgin of Israel: thou shalt again be adorned with thy tabrets, and shalt go forth in the dances of them that make merry. Thou shalt yet plant vines upon the mountains of Samaria: the planters shall plant, and shall eat them as common things. For there shall be a day, that the watchmen upon the mount Ephraim shall cry, Arise ye, and let us go up to Zion unto the LORD our God.

You may be in captivity now, but the Lord still loves you with an everlasting love. So just hold on because your life isn't over. He will build you up again. He will plant things in your life again. Trust in him. If you've written it all down, the day will come when you will look back and say, "Thank you, Jesus, for bringing me back home to you!"

God, I don't understand what I'm going through right now, but I know you still love me. I'm ready to be built up again. I'm ready to have things planted in my life again. Set me free and bring me home to you, Lord.

Jeremiah 31:25–26
For I have satiated the weary soul, and I have replenished every sorrowful soul. Upon this I awaked, and beheld; and my sleep was sweet unto me.

The Hebrew word for "satiated" can mean intoxicated, but in this context, it means soaked or saturated with water. If your soul is weary and thirsty, God will give you more water than you can hold. If you're sorry for your sin and repent, God will give you more good things than you can contain: peace, pardon, righteousness, salvation, the Spirit, spiritual gifts, the gospel, and so on. Through this and this alone can you find rest.

Lord, I'm weary with life and thirsty for you. Please give me living water to drink. Lord, I am sorry for my sin and I repent before you. I look forward with gratefulness to all the good things you are going to add to my life. Now that my life is replenished, I won't worry anymore. I pray that you will give me rest tonight.

Jeremiah 31:33
But this shall be the covenant that I will make with the house of Israel; After those days, saith the LORD, I will put my law in their inward parts, and write it in their hearts; and will be their God, and they shall be my people.

The writer of Hebrews referenced the high priest entering into the Holy of Holies once a year to offer the blood of an animal as a sacrifice for the sin of the people. He wrote, "Christ did not enter into a holy place made with human hands, which was only a copy of the true one in heaven . . . and he did not offer himself again and again, like the High Priest here on earth who enters the Most Holy Place year after year with the blood of an animal

. . . Now, once for all time, he has appeared at the end of the age to remove sin by his own death as a sacrifice" (Heb. 9:24–26 NLT).

Jeremiah 31:31–34 introduces a new covenant—a covenant written upon our hearts. When we enter into this covenant, we become members of the family of God. We should constantly thank God for the new covenant he provided for us on Calvary.

Jesus, thank you for offering yourself on Calvary and instituting this new covenant. I choose to live by the terms of this covenant all the days of my life.

Jeremiah 32:39–42
And I will give them one heart, and one way, that they may fear me for ever, for the good of them, and of their children after them: and I will make an everlasting covenant with them, that I will not turn away from them, to do them good; but I will put my fear in their hearts, that they shall not depart from me. Yea, I will rejoice over them to do them good, and

> *I will plant them in this land assuredly with my whole heart and with my whole soul. For thus saith the LORD; Like as I have brought all this great evil upon this people, so will I bring upon them all the good that I have promised them.*

The promises of God are innumerable and immutable. Just as the Lord had promised to punish his people because of their sin, he also promised that he would bless the people with all the good things he had in store for them. To further ensure that this would come to pass, God promised to put "his fear in their hearts." The fear of the Lord is simply "submit[ting] to His sovereign majesty and walk[ing] according to His way" (The Nelson Study Bible). God is not a harsh dictator, but he does require that we respect him and his rules as a child does the rules of a good father.

The Lord will rejoice over you as you live according to this new covenant. He will plant you in a good land and grant you all the good things he has promised to his children. He is a good father.

Father, I thank you for your goodness toward me. You have planned everything for my life according to your timing. I fear you and trust in the good promises you have for my life.

Jeremiah 33:1–3
Moreover the word of the LORD came unto Jeremiah the second time, while he was yet shut up in the court of the prison, saying, Thus saith the LORD the maker thereof, the LORD that formed it, to establish it; the LORD is his name; Call unto me, and I will answer thee, and show thee great and mighty things, which thou knowest not.

It happened in the tenth year of Zedekiah's reign while Jerusalem was suffering through a Babylonian siege. Zedekiah was extremely agitated with Jeremiah because he had prophesied the city would fall to the Babylonians. Jeremiah assured the king that no matter how much resistance he was able to muster, he would not succeed against the Babylonians. He would be carted off to Babylon and come face to face with the dreadful Nebuchadnezzar.

These "seditious speeches" of Jeremiah so enraged Zedekiah that he had the prophet arrested and thrown into prison.

Shut away from everyone, Jeremiah must have felt hopeless and abandoned. God had called him and given him messages for the people of Judah, but they had hated him for it and inflicted much pain and suffering upon him. Why was God allowing all of these bad things to come upon him? All he was doing was trying to obey the Lord.

Even prison couldn't stop the word of the Lord from coming to Jeremiah. The Lord showed up and reminded the weeping prophet that *he* was the mighty Creator who had formed the earth and established it. He told Jeremiah to cry out to him, and he would show him "great and unsearchable things" he didn't yet know (NLT).

There is nothing like the voice of the Lord coming to you in the middle of your trial. Even in the prison of your circumstances the Lord can show you great and unsearchable things. All you have to do is call out to him.

Lord, I call out to you. I may be in a prison, but you are still the Lord over my circumstances. Show me great and unsearchable things, I pray.

Jeremiah 38:10
Then the king commanded Ebed-melech the Ethiopian, saying, Take from hence thirty men with thee, and take up Jeremiah the prophet out of the dungeon, before he die.

When Pharoah's army marched north out of Egypt, the Babylonians abandoned their siege of Jerusalem to deal with the threat. Meanwhile, Jeremiah decided to go to Anathoth, located about three miles northeast of Jerusalem, where he had purchased a field from his cousin. He had just reached the Gate of Benjamin when he was met by Irijah, captain of the guard, who accused him of defecting to the Babylonians. Jeremiah protested, "No, I'm not defecting! I'm just trying to go home!" But they arrested him and brought him to the princes, who ordered that he be lowered by ropes into a dungeon.

This dungeon was a basement cistern in the house of Malchiah the king's son. Probably due to the lengthy siege, the cistern had no water fit for drinking, and the bottom of the cistern was deep in slime. Verse 6 says Jeremiah "sank in the mire." "The court princes probably expected Jeremiah to die a slow and quiet death" in that cistern (The Nelson Study Bible) and were looking forward to the time they wouldn't have to listen to the prophet's harangues anymore.

The king owned an Ethiopian slave named Ebed-melech, who was a eunuch. Now Ethiopians had a terrible reputation for cruelty, but Ebed-melech was different. "He was as faithful a servant to God as he was to King Zedekiah. He loved the prophet Jeremiah and risked his own life to save the man of God" (Herbert Lockyer, *All the Men of the Bible*).

Ebed-melech went to the king and pleaded that Jeremiah be set free. The king complied. Ebed-melech and thirty men lifted the prophet out of the dungeon with ropes wrapped in rags for padding.

After the Babylonians had regrouped and finally broke through the Jerusalem wall, Nebuchadnezzar told his captain to find Jeremiah and "see that he isn't hurt. Look after him well, and give him anything he wants" (Jer. 39:12, NLT). Unbelievably, the enemy treated Jeremiah better than his own people!

Ebed-melech's loyalty to God had given him courage to approach the king. His kindness put Jeremiah's cruel enemies to shame. He did Jeremiah a great service by using simple, weak things—rags and cords. Because of these acts of kindness toward Jeremiah, Ebed-melech received a blessing of protection.

The prayer here is to lift up your prophet, the man or woman of God in your life. You may not realize how much they need your prayers, support, and encouragement. For example, Jeremiah was alone in his stand for God. He was not allowed to marry. His family turned against him. The people hated him and didn't believe him. He was not allowed to mourn for loved ones, go to feasts, or attend parties. (See Jer. 16.) He was left alone to bear the horrifying knowledge of impending judgment on God's people.

Don't let your prophet rot in a dungeon! Lift him or her up! Your own protection and blessings rely on your treatment of your prophet.

God, I will lift up the prophets you have placed in my life. I pray for them right now. I will encourage and support them. I will protect them at all costs.

Jeremiah 42:4–6
Then Jeremiah the prophet said unto them, I have heard you; behold, I will pray unto the Lord your God according to your words; and it shall come to pass, that whatsoever thing the Lord shall answer you, I will declare it unto you; I will keep nothing back from you. Then they said to Jeremiah, The Lord be a true and faithful witness between us, if we do not even according to all things for the which the Lord thy God shall send thee to us. Whether it be good, or whether it be evil, we will obey the voice of the Lord our God, to whom we send thee; that it may be well with us, when we obey the voice of the Lord our God.

Certain nobles and common people who still remained in Jerusalem came to Jeremiah and said, "Pray that the LORD your God will tell us where we should go and what we should do" (v. 3, NIV). They promised, "Whether it is favorable or unfavorable, we will obey the LORD our God, to whom we are sending you, so that it will go well with us, for we will obey the LORD our God" (Jer. 42:6, NIV).

Jeremiah did as they requested, and ten days later came back with this reply from the Lord: "If you stay in this land, I will build you up and not tear you down; I will plant you and not uproot you, for I have relented concerning the disaster I have inflicted on you" (v. 10, NIV). But that wasn't all. The Lord said if the people refused to listen and defected to Egypt anyway, the same horrific things that had happened in Jerusalem would happen to them in Egypt.

The people turned on Jeremiah and accused him of being a false prophet. They packed up and left for Egypt, taking Jeremiah with them. The prophet probably died while still in Egypt.

Chapter 44 is a record of Jeremiah's last message, and it was directed to all the Jews living in

Egypt: "I will take away the remnant of Judah who were determined to go to Egypt and settle there. They will all perish in Egypt; they will fall by the sword or die of famine" (44:12, NIV).

Too many people come to their pastor or other godly influencer in their lives, seeking advice. Like this Jewish remnant, some even say they will do what the Lord indicates is his will, even if they don't like it. Unfortunately, many already have made up their minds to do what they want no matter what advice is given. They feel that because they want to do that thing or move to that place, it surely must be the Lord's will. Then, when the true advice comes, they get mad and do what they want anyway, usually to their own detriment. Sadly, their decision affects not only themselves but their family, friends, and those in their circle of influence.

Lord, help me not to have the attitude of the people who asked Jeremiah for advice. I want my heart be pure before you so that I will trust whatever you say whether I like it or not, whether it feels good or bad, for I know you have it all in control. And if I obey your

word, I know that all will be well with me and my family. In Jesus' name, amen.

Jeremiah 50:6
My people hath been lost sheep: their shepherds have caused them to go astray, they have turned them away on the mountains: they have gone from mountain to hill, they have forgotten their restingplace.

Jeremiah registered several indictments against the shepherds (pastors or priests) of Judah and Israel. In 2:8, he said the pastors had transgressed against the Lord by their mishandling of the Law. In 10:21, he accused the pastors of becoming "brutish," which indicates they were foolish, reckless, persistently ignorant, and dangerous. The shepherds were ignorant because they didn't inquire of the Lord or consult his word. In 12:10, the Lord accused the pastors of destroying his vineyard; and in 50:6, the Lord lamented that his people were like lost sheep because the shepherds had caused them to go astray.

All of this highlights your urgent need of a good shepherd. Pray for the pastor in your life, the one who will lead you down the right paths. (For a more complete description of a good shepherd, see the section on Psalm 23 in Book 2 of the Road to Relationship series: *Praying the Word: Psalms, Proverbs, and Ecclesiastes*.)

Lord, I thank you that you are the Good Shepherd who cares for the sheep. I pray for my pastor, your under-shepherd. Help him not to lead me astray, but rather to lead me toward you. Amen.

LAMENTATIONS

Lamentations 3:17–32

And thou hast removed my soul far off from peace: I forgat prosperity. And I said, My strength and my hope is perished from the LORD: remembering mine affliction and my misery, the wormwood and the gall. My soul hath them still in remembrance, and is humbled in me. This I recall to my mind, therefore have I hope. It is of the LORD's mercies that we are not consumed, because his compassions fail not. They are new every morning: great is thy faithfulness. The LORD is my portion, saith my soul; therefore will I hope in him. The LORD is good unto them that wait for him, to the soul that seeketh him. It is good that a man should both hope and quietly wait for the salvation of the LORD. It is good for a man that he bear the yoke in his youth. He sitteth alone and keepeth silence, because he hath borne it upon him. He putteth his mouth in the dust; if so be there may be hope. He giveth his cheek to him that smiteth him: he is filled full with reproach. For the LORD will not cast off for ever: but though he cause grief, yet will he have compassion according to the multitude of his mercies.

I began with verse 17 in order to set the scene. Nebuchadnezzar's hordes had looted and burned the city of Jerusalem, killing thousands, stripping away peace and prosperity, and leaving suffering and homelessness in their wake. No wonder Jeremiah is called the weeping prophet. He invested forty years of ministry warning the people of coming destruction if they didn't turn to the Lord. Now that the destruction had come to pass, he was left to mourn.

Tradition attributes the authorship of Lamentations to Jeremiah. The book "is a collection of five poems . . . [that] express heart-wrenching grief and sorrow, remorse for the sin that caused the downfall of Judah, and a yet undying hope in God's covenant faithfulness" (Apostolic Study Bible). "Chapters 1 and 5 provide summaries of the siege and fall of Jerusalem, while chapters 2 and 4 offer more detailed and explicit description of the devastation" (The Nelson Study Bible).

Thus, reading Lamentations can be quite depressing. However, right in the middle of this doom and gloom is chapter 3—a golden nugget with Jeremiah's beautiful description of the Lord's mercy and faithfulness that "constitute[s] one of the most poignant expressions of faith in all of Scripture" (Apostolic Study Bible). My Bible titles this section "Remembering God's Faithfulness." Jeremiah recounts the Lord's mercies, his faithful, undying love, and his goodness to all those who search for him.

Verse 21 says, "This I recall to my mind, therefore have I hope." Stan Gleason said in his book *The Unflawed Leader,* "It's been said that a person can live forty days without food, four days without water, four minutes without air, but only four seconds without hope." Brian Kinsey stated in *Made for More,* "Remember that hope is not spiritually given. It is purposefully driven."

Do you remember a time in your life when it seemed like everything had come crashing down around you—like someone had pulled the rug out from under you? When all your peace and prosperity had been snatched away, leaving you with only bitter dregs? When it seemed God had removed his kindness from your life? How does one find hope in the middle of all that? By doing the same things Jeremiah did: (1) he remembered the faithfulness of God; (2) he rejoiced in the Lord's mercies, for they are new every morning; and (3) he recalled biblical passages to mind. All of this caused hope to spring up for Jeremiah, and it will for you too!

Lord, in my darkest lament, I will activate my hope by remembering your faithfulness to me, rejoicing in your mercy, and recalling favorite passages in your word. In Jesus' name.

EZEKIEL

Ezekiel 2:5

And they, whether they will hear, or whether they will forbear, (for they are a rebellious house,) yet shall know that there hath been a prophet among them.

Ezekiel, who was a priest, received his call to prophetic ministry in 593 BC, six years before the Babylonian Captivity. He was among the first group of Jews to be deported to Babylon in 587 BC. There Ezekiel saw a vision of the glory of the Lord by the Chebar River, a tributary of the mighty Euphrates. Jewish settlements were along this river in the land between the Tigris and Euphrates Rivers.

Like Jeremiah, Ezekiel had a tough task before him. He told the people of God they had brought the suffering upon themselves through their betrayal of God. This young prophet was to faithfully deliver the words of the Lord without being afraid of the people's response or what they might do to him. In 2:5 (NIV), the Lord told Ezekiel, "Whether they listen or fail to listen—for they are a rebellious people—they will know that a prophet has been among them."

Our responsibility as ministers of the gospel is simply to speak the word of the Lord—both his written word and what he reveals to us through prayer. God doesn't ask us to *save* anyone; only he can do that. However, everyone has an opportunity to accept the word or reject it. Whether or not they are saved is up to them. Therefore, our job is to obey God when he asks us to speak, and to pray that people will turn their hearts toward the Lord after the word is spoken.

God, when you give me a word, I will not back down from my assignment. However, I am not responsible for people's reactions to the word I speak. They can either reject it or receive it. In the end, help them to realize there was an effort made to reach them, and that a minister of your gospel was among them. In Jesus' name.

Ezekiel 3:10

Moreover he said unto me, Son of man, all my words that I shall speak unto thee receive in thine heart, and hear with thine ears.

Lord, I will receive every word you speak to me and hide it in my heart.

Ezekiel 3:20–21

Again, When a righteous man doth turn from his righteousness, and commit iniquity, and I lay a stumblingblock before him, he shall die: because thou hast not given him warning, he shall die in his sin, and his righteousness which he hath done shall not be remembered; but his blood will I require at thine hand. Nevertheless if thou warn the righteous man, that the righteous sin not, and he doth not sin, he shall surely live, because he is warned; also thou hast delivered thy soul.

In Ezekiel 33: 7, the Lord told this prophet he was a watchman over the house of Israel. He was to hear what the Lord said, and in turn speak the word to the people. If he failed to warn the wicked and they subsequently died, their blood would be on Ezekiel's hands. But if Ezekiel preached the warning and the people obeyed and lived, Ezekiel's own soul would be delivered.

Being a watchman of the Lord is serious business, whether for a prophet in the Old Testament or a present-day minister. God requires his watchmen to *do something.*

You are a watchman. When God tells you to do something, don't wait. Because the more you ignore his voice, the less you will be able to discern it. Yes, it is the voice of God telling you to pray more. Yes, it is the voice of God calling you to deepen your relationship with him. Yes, it is the voice of God telling you to invite your coworker to church. Yes, it is the voice of God telling you to give your testimony to the friend you meet at the grocery store. Yes, it is the voice of God telling you to ask someone if they would like to study the Bible with you (cf. Ezek. 44:23).

If you listen to and obey the voice of God, you not only will be the means of saving others, but you yourself will be saved.

Lord, I will listen to what you want me to do and will perform it. And I pray that through my effort to speak your word to others, that they will be saved.

Ezekiel 7:14
They have blown the trumpet, even to make all ready; but none goeth to the battle: for my wrath is upon all the multitude thereof.

Lord, when it is time for me to enter spiritual warfare, I will be ready. When my pastor declares it is time to war against the enemy, I will be on the front lines.

Ezekiel 11:19–20
And I will give them one heart, and I will put a new spirit within you; and I will take the stony heart out of their flesh, and will give them an heart of flesh: that they may walk in my statutes, and keep mine ordinances, and do them: and they shall be my people, and I will be their God.

These verses parallel Ezekiel 36:26–27 (NKJV): "I will give you a new heart and put a new spirit within you; I will take the heart of stone out of your flesh and give you a heart of flesh. I will put My Spirit within you and cause you to walk in My statutes, and you will keep My judgments and do them."

The above passages are alluded to in Jesus' conversation with Nicodemus about being born again from above through the new birth—being born of water and of the Spirit (John 3:3, 5). Ezekiel's writing "presages God's cleansing of human hearts with water and their inner transformation by His Spirit" (*Commentary on the New Testament Use of the Old Testament*).

For someone who needs a transformation, a new start on life, this is your verse. Whether your past trouble has been of your own doing or someone else has turned your heart to stone, God is your Redeemer. He will give you a new heart and will place his Spirit within you. Peter preached about this inner transformation (Acts 2), quoting from the prophet Joel (Acts 2:16–18), and instructing the people on how to be born of water and of the Spirit (Acts 2:38). Peter added that the Lord's promise, delivered through his prophets, is for everyone (Acts 2:39)!

Trust in the Lord's redemptive power.

God, I ask you to redeem me. Transform my heart and place your Spirit within me. In Jesus' name.

Ezekiel 16:60
Nevertheless I will remember my covenant with thee in the days of thy youth, and I will establish unto thee an everlasting covenant.

Amazingly, although Israel had committed gross sins for centuries, God was willing to renew the "everlasting covenant" he had established with Abraham (Gen. 17:7–8). This meant that if the people would put their lives back together by once again obeying the terms of the covenant, God would renew it. Forgiveness is powerful, and, thankfully, God is always quick to forgive.

Ezekiel 16:63 (ESV) says, "That you may . . . never open your mouth again because of your shame, when I atone you for all that you have done, declares the Lord GOD." Israel would be ashamed when they finally realized the contrast between their extreme unfaithfulness and God's faithfulness. But God didn't want them to be ashamed forever. He wanted them to obey the terms of the covenant because they loved him and trusted in his forgiveness.

God does not want you to live in shame, but rather in covenant with him. When you violate the terms of your covenant with God, you incur shame, but as long as you will repent and come back to that covenant, God will accept you.

Our covenant today is the gospel—the death, burial, and resurrection of Jesus Christ (1 Cor. 15:1–4). Our salvation experience should parallel his death, burial, and resurrection; namely, in repentance (death to sin), burial (being immersed in water for the remission of sin), and receiving the Spirit (rising to walk in newness of life).

God, I want to live according to your covenant all the days of my life. I will not walk in shame because of my past; rather, I will ask for and accept your forgiveness. I want to be in covenant with you.

Ezekiel 33:5

He heard the sound of the trumpet, and took not warning; his blood shall be upon him. But he that taketh warning shall deliver his soul.

Just as in Ezekiel's day, we are given many warning signs that Jesus is coming soon. If you don't believe me, read Matthew 24. It's almost like reading today's newspaper! We don't want to be like the Israelites who did not heed their prophets' warnings. Take heed to the warnings in the Bible and deliver your soul!

I will receive your warnings, Jesus. You are coming soon, and I want to be ready.

Ezekiel 37:1–10

The hand of the Lord was upon me, and carried me out in the spirit of the Lord, and set me down in the midst of the valley which was full of bones, and caused me to pass by them round about: and, behold, there were very many in the open valley; and, lo, they were very dry. And he said unto me, Son of man, can these bones live? And I answered, O Lord God, thou knowest. Again he said unto me, Prophesy upon these bones, and say unto them, O ye dry bones, hear the word of the LORD. Thus saith the Lord GOD unto these bones; Behold, I will cause breath to enter into you, and ye shall live: and I will lay sinews upon you, and will bring up flesh upon you, and cover you with skin, and put breath in you, and ye shall live; and ye shall know that I am the LORD. So I prophesied as I was commanded: and as I prophesied, there was a noise, and behold a shaking, and the bones came together, bone to his bone. And when I beheld, lo, the sinews and the flesh came up upon them, and the skin covered them above: but there was no breath in them. Then said he unto me, Prophesy unto the wind, prophesy, son of man, and say to the wind, Thus saith the Lord GOD; Come from the four winds, O breath, and breathe upon these slain, that they may live. So I prophesied as he commanded me, and the breath came into them, and they lived, and stood up upon their feet, an exceeding great army.

Ezekiel's ministry seems to have three phases: (1) judgment upon sinful Judah (1:1–24:27); (2) judgment against surrounding nations (25:1–32:32); and (3) the restoration of Israel (33:1–48:35).

"In January of 585 BC, five months after the temple had been destroyed, a fugitive delivered the news to Ezekiel. . . . Now that Ezekiel's prophecies of judgment had been fulfilled, his ministry would be primarily one of encouragement, and his messages would focus on the future restoration of the exiles. . . . Ezekiel's vision of the dry bones portrayed in a vivid way Israel's miraculous restoration" (*Holman Bible Handbook*).

Ezekiel's valley of dry bones is one of the most iconic scenes in the prophetic books. In fact, it was, in part, the inspiration for the cover of this book. I'm going to break down this passage and give several different models of prayers we can pray.

The Spirit of the Lord carried Ezekiel to a deserted valley. How he got there is important, because we often think we must have done something wrong to end up in such an awful place. But many people throughout the Bible were led, carried, or driven to a desolate place (e.g., Moses, Ezekiel, Elijah, John the Baptist, Philip, Paul, and Jesus come to mind).

The bones Ezekiel saw in this valley weren't just a little dry; they were *very* dry. The NLT says "completely dried out," which, science tells us, means they had to have been lying there at least a year, probably much longer. There were enough disconnected bones to cover the whole floor of the valley.

Ezekiel must have been a bit confused. Why would the Spirit bring him to such a strange place? He found out later that the bones represented God's people "who had been dead and scattered so long that their hope had dried up" (Apostolic Study Bible). (See Ezek. 37:11–14.)

The Lord asked Ezekiel, "Can these bones live?" Ezekiel possibly shrugged his shoulders. "Only you would know that, Lord. I sure don't. They look awful dry to me."

I'd like to stop here and introduce a prayer. When God leads, drives, or carries us to a desolate valley, our best response is to simply say, "Lord, you know the plan, so I will trust you." Ezekiel didn't understand, but he knew that God had a good reason for putting him in that valley.

Lord, when you lead me to a dry, desolate place, I will not become confused and frustrated. Instead, I will simply trust you and your plan for my life.

God then commanded Ezekiel to prophesy to the bones. What does it mean to prophesy? It means to speak the word of the Lord! Speak life—that is, positive things. Speak out loud what God has told you in prayer. It may be difficult to speak to a "dead" thing. It will require stirring up your faith in God. But the word of the Lord brings life every time!

Lord, I will prophesy in the dry valley where you brought me. I will not question your word, but I will speak life!

Ezekiel preached to the bones exactly what the Lord had told him to say. "Listen here, you bones! I don't care how long you've been lying there. When you hear the word of the Lord, tendons are going to appear, muscle is going to attach, and skin is going to cover your flesh!" Sure enough, as Ezekiel continued to prophesy to the bones, tendons, muscle, and skin appeared. But the bodies were still lying there lifeless. Ezekiel then said, "Come, O breath, from the four winds! Breathe into these dead bodies so they may live again" (37:9, NLT). And the bodies came to life and stood up.

Evangelist Billy Cole said, "Speak what you seek until you see what you say!" The essence of revival is believing that dead things will be revived. Let's examine this process.

Bone coming to bone signifies unity—coming together as a body. After the bones came together and grew flesh and skin, there were enough bodies to make up a great army.

Unity is the first step in the revival process. When the body begins to unite, you can be sure something great is on the horizon. An army is being formed.

Elders and young people must be in unity. Men and women and families must be in unity. All ethnicities must be in unity. Pastors and ministry teams and saints must be in unity. Churches across town must be in unity. God's kingdom as a whole should constantly pursue unity.

God, unify us! Unify my family, my church, and your kingdom as a whole. Let unity be our first step toward revival!

After sinews (tendons) appeared, muscle began to form. We fight not against flesh and blood, but against principalities, powers, rulers of darkness, and wickedness in high places (Eph. 6:12). Our muscle is our prayer. If we as a church will unite together and pray together, nothing will be able to stop us. We must pray. There is no other alternative.

God, stir up a spirit of prayer in my family, church, and your kingdom as a whole. Let us unite together in prayer for revival around the globe.

Next comes the skin. When people look at the army, they see the skin, not the sinews or the bones or the muscles (unity and prayer). How do others in your school, workplace, or community view you? Sure, they see your outward appearance, but much more. They see the way you conduct yourself. They see your character. They see how you treat others. Work on having a holy appearance and holy "conversation," which, in the KJV, means behavior. "Our manner of life should reflect holiness because God is holy" (Aretha Grant, ibelieve.com, 2018).

However, this "skin" is not just for looks only. Just as human skin is our first line of defense against germs trying to enter our body, holiness is our first line of defense against the enemy's attacks. Let your conversation and appearance be appropriate for the army of God.

Lord, I will conduct myself in a holy way before you. Let my appearance be acceptable in your eyes.

Finally, breath entered the dead bodies and the army came alive! Likewise, many people may come together in unity, try to exemplify good character, and even pray, but they lack the Spirit—which is the most important thing. We must prophesy to the wind and allow the Spirit of the Lord to sweep out every dead thing in our lives. The Spirit brings life! And when your church combines the Spirit with unity, prayer, and holy living, an army will arise!

Let your Spirit sweep over me, my family, my church, and your kingdom, Lord. Breathe into me. Let your Spirit speak life. I will prophesy in the Spirit, and we will have revival.

Ezekiel 44:9
Thus saith the Lord God; No stranger, uncircumcised in heart, nor uncircumcised in flesh, shall enter into my sanctuary, of any stranger that is among the children of Israel.

This verse is interesting to pray about, but first we need a little background. In Ezekiel 10, the prophet saw the glory of the Lord gradually depart from Solomon's Temple because of the people's idolatry and sin. Then the Babylonians overthrew Jerusalem, destroyed the temple, burned it to the ground, and carted off its gold and treasures to Babylon.

Fast-forward to the twenty-fifth year of Israel's captivity. The Lord took Ezekiel on a virtual tour of a new temple in Jerusalem and let the prophet know that certain practices in the preexilic temple would not be tolerated in the new temple. For instance, in preexilic times, foreigners—those out of covenant with God—had been allowed to have leadership and participation in the temple. There is even some speculation that priests may have hired others to do their work or may even have taken bribes from people who were eager to serve in the temple. The Lord said that in the new temple, only those who were circumcised in heart and flesh would be allowed to serve.

The physical sign that Jews were in covenant with the Lord was circumcision. But circumcision of the heart was—and still is—essential. In Romans 2:29 Paul wrote, "He is a Jew, which is one inwardly; and circumcision is that of the heart, in the spirit, and not in the letter."

Circumcision of the heart involves repentance—confessing one's sins to God, asking for forgiveness, and turning away from sin—and loving

God with all one's heart and soul. Then, like David, we can look forward to dwelling in the house of the Lord forever (Psalm 23:6).

Lord, I repent of my sins today and ask that you will circumcise my heart so I may enter into relationship with you. I want to dwell in your sanctuary daily.

Ezekiel 44:23
And they shall teach my people the difference between the holy and profane, and cause them to discern between the unclean and the clean.

A person's conscience is supposed to help them discern the difference between right and wrong. However, this world is blurring the lines through humanism and situation ethics. We need to study God's word and pray that he will teach us the difference between the holy and profane, the clean and unclean.

Jesus, help me to be aware of the deception in the world through humanism and situation ethics. You

are my truth, Lord, not the polluted idea of truth that is prevalent in the world today. I want to follow the guidelines in your word for that which is holy and clean in your sight. Amen.

Ezekiel 44:28
And it shall be unto them for an inheritance: I am their inheritance: and ye shall give them no possession in Israel: I am their possession.

Under the law, priests and Levites were not allotted portions of land for their inheritance. Instead, the Lord was to be their possession. This meant they had no income from raising crops or running secular businesses; ministering to the Lord was their business. If the people were obeying the law, the priests and Levites enjoyed abundant provision through the people's tithes and the sacrificial system.

Peter wrote, "You are a chosen people. You are royal priests, a holy nation, God's very own possession. As a result, you can show others the goodness of God, for he has called you out of darkness into this wonderful light" (1 Pet. 2:9, NLT). Peter indicated that God's children are "sojourners and pilgrims" (1 Pet. 2:11, NKJV). A sojourner is someone who stays temporarily. We don't "own property" in this world; instead, a wonderful inheritance awaits us in Heaven, for we are "joint-heirs with Christ" (Rom. 8:16–17; see also Gal. 4:7).

Lord, you are my everything—my glorious inheritance and my prized possession in life. I love you with all my heart.

Ezekiel 46:13
Thou shalt daily prepare a burnt offering unto the Lord of a lamb of the first year without blemish: thou shalt prepare it every morning.

Here we see the familiar words *daily* and *every morning*. While we no longer prepare literal burnt offerings of a lamb every morning, we do offer a sacrifice. Romans 12:1 (NLT) says, "I plead with you to give your bodies to God because of all he has done for you. Let them be a living and holy sacrifice—the kind he will find acceptable. This is truly the way to worship him."

When you wake up in the morning and lay your flesh (carnal nature) on the altar through repentance, you are enacting the New Testament fulfillment of this verse in Ezekiel.

Lord, I will lay myself on the altar every morning. I give myself to you as a living sacrifice. I desire to be holy and acceptable in your sight. Amen.

Ezekiel 47:3–5

And when the man that had the line in his hand went forth eastward, he measured a thousand cubits, and he brought me through the waters; the waters were to the ankles. Again he measured a thousand, and brought me through the waters; the waters were to the knees. Again he measured a thousand, and brought me through; the waters were to the loins. Afterward he measured a thousand; and it was a river that I could not pass over: for the waters were risen, waters to swim in, a river that could not be passed over.

God gave Ezekiel a vision of a river that will flow out from underneath the house of the Lord in Jerusalem during the millennium. Bible commentator Warren Wiersbe wrote, "Jerusalem is the only city of the ancient world that wasn't located on a river, and in the [Mideast], a dependable water supply is essential for life and for defense. During the Kingdom Age, Jerusalem shall have a river such as no other nation ever had."

Ezekiel kept following the man who was measuring the river, and within a mile it went from a small trickle to waist deep, finally becoming so deep that Ezekiel couldn't go any further without swimming.

This should help us realize that we can't continue to dabble in shallow waters when it comes to praying, reading the word, or knowing God. We should desire more than just a little bit of Bible knowledge, a tiny portion of God's Spirit, or a few seconds of prayer. Instead, we should desire "waters to swim in."

God, take me deeper in your word and in your Spirit. I don't want my relationship with you to be shallow.

I want to spend time with you every day until I am swimming in the living waters of your Spirit.

Ezekiel 47:9
And it shall come to pass, that every thing that liveth, which moveth, whithersoever the rivers shall come, shall live: and there shall be a very great multitude of fish, because these waters shall come thither: for they shall be healed; and every thing shall live whither the river cometh.

This verse is near and dear to my heart because it contains our church's theme. We are the River of Life, and our theme is "Where the river flows, everything shall live."

Jesus said in John 7:37–39, "If any man thirst, let him come unto me, and drink. He that believeth on me, as the scripture hath said, out of his belly shall flow rivers of living water. (But this spake he of the Spirit, which they that believe on him should receive." Jesus was referring to a composite of Old Testament texts, including Isaiah 44:3; Ezekiel 47:9; Joel 2:28–29; and Zechariah 14:8. As indicated by the parenthetical phrase in John 7:39, the outpouring of the Spirit ("rivers of living water") did not take place until after Jesus' glorification.

If the Spirit of the Lord dwells in you, you are a river of life. As the temple of the Holy Ghost (I Cor. 6:19–20), you contain the same healing waters that Ezekiel saw flowing from beneath the temple. Therefore, walk worthy of the vocation to which you are called (Eph. 4:1). What is this vocation? It is to be a river! Let the Spirit flow through you in all areas, every day, to all people. Wherever you go things should live and not die. The Spirit in you should speak life to others, healing to others, encouragement to others. Be the river of life!

Lord, I will be the river of life. I will not keep your Spirit all to myself, but I will let the waters of life flow to others through my speech and actions. I will be the river.

DANIEL

Daniel 1:6–7

Now among these were of the children of Judah, Daniel, Hananiah, Mishael, and Azariah: unto whom the prince of the eunuchs gave names: for he gave unto Daniel the name of Belteshazzar; and to Hananiah, of Shadrach; and to Mishael, of Meshach; and to Azariah, of Abednego.

Four young Jewish men, Daniel, Hananiah, Mishael, and Azariah, were deported to Babylon in 606 BC during the three-month reign of King Jehoiachin. Jerusalem had fallen, and about ten thousand of Judah's professionals, priests, craftsmen, and the wealthy (Jewish Virtual Library) were deported to Babylon. According to Herbert Lockyer in *All the Men of the Bible*, Daniel was about fifteen years old, and it can be assumed his three friends were young as well. Being deported was the first step in the loss of identity for these young men.

The second step was that as soon as they arrived in Babylon, they were "placed in the care of the chief of the eunuchs" (1:7, ESV and NKJV). "The Hebrew word is *saris*, a specific word used to describe a man in the ancient world who had been emasculated in order to fulfill a religious or government role" (Christopher R. Smith, Good Questions). One clue that these young men were made eunuchs is found in Isaiah when the prophet addressed two groups of people among the returning exiles who were wondering if they had any place in the restored community of Israel. (See the section on Isaiah 56:1–5.) Eunuchs comprised one of these groups.

The third step to loss of identity was that the chief of the eunuchs gave them Babylonish names. Hananiah ("Yah protects") was renamed Shadrach ("circuit of the sun"). Mishael ("who is like the mighty One") was renamed Meshach ("who is what Aku is," mocking Israel's God). Azariah ("Yah will help") was renamed Abednego ("servant of Nebo," a Babylonian deity).

Despite being torn from their homes, placed in an alien environment, robbed of their ability to have children, and denied their Hebrew names, these teenagers never lost their relationship with Jehovah nor denied their Jewish heritage.

We live in an alien world. As soon as we walk outside the doors of the church, we are in foreign territory because we are "in this world, but not of this world." Paul urged the Roman Christians, "Do not conform to the pattern of this world, but be transformed by the renewing of your mind" (Rom. 12:2, NIV). Bible scholar J. B. Phillips stated the verse metaphorically: "Don't let the world around you squeeze you into its own mould, but let God re-make you so that your whole attitude of mind is changed" (*The New Testament in Modern English*).

The world will try to change your identity by relocating you (orienting you to their world), labeling you, expecting you to play by their rules, and thus robbing you of your relationship with God. You do not have to bow down to the things of this world! You do not have to think like them, dress like them, talk like them, or go where they go. Hold fast to your true identity in God by having a renewed mind—renewed in repentance, in reading the word of God, and in keeping your covenant with him up to date.

God, despite the world's attempts to change my identity, I choose to live in relationship with you. I choose to follow your way. Though this world may call me names, I will stand true to your word.

Daniel 1:9
Now God had brought Daniel into favour and tender love with the prince of the eunuchs.

The NIV says, "Now God had caused the official to show favor and compassion to Daniel." A further study of the life of Daniel shows that he not only had the respect and compassion of the Babylonian official, but he went on to find favor with the political leaders of one of the largest kingdoms to ever exist. He was active throughout the reign of Nebuchadnezzar (604–562 BC), and was still in Babylon when Cyrus, the Persian, captured Babylon. He became a high-ranking government official during the reigns of Cyrus (539–529 BC) and Cambyses (529–522 BC), and also served during his old age into the reign of Darius I (522–486 BC).

Why did he have such favor among these pagan rulers? Because God brought him into favor. Don't mistake the hand of God on your life when he is trying to connect you to powerful people in your community. The Bible says Daniel was shown "tender love" (compassion) by people in authority. We as Christians need to pray for the leaders in our community instead of criticizing them. Paul wrote, "I exhort therefore, that, first of all, supplications, prayers, intercessions, and giving of thanks, be made for all men; for kings, and for all that are in authority; that we may lead a quiet and peaceable life in all godliness and honesty" (1 Tim. 1:1–2). If we start loving, praying for, and supporting those in government leadership, we may find God bringing us into their favor.

Daniel's favor saved his friends' lives as well as his own many times. It made the people of God prosperous, allowed for dreams and visions to be interpreted, and so much more. Seek favor from the Lord with your community leaders.

Lord, I pray for the leaders in my community, asking that you will bring me into favor and tender love (compassion) with these leaders so they might make right decisions, and that Christians will continue to be able to worship you freely.

Daniel 1:17
As for these four children, God gave them knowledge and skill in all learning and wisdom: and Daniel had understanding in all visions and dreams.

Daniel, Hananiah, Azariah, and Mishael were gifted young men. They not only were skilled in all learning and wisdom, but Daniel had the God-given ability to interpret visions. These gifts were beneficial to God's people as well as the Babylonian kingdom.

God gives you gifts for a reason—to be used in the church, in your community, and on your job, with the end goal of reaching for others and developing relationships. So expect giftings. Expect promotions. Expect to excel in life. But ultimately use your gifts for the kingdom.

God, I pray that you will gift me in all learning and wisdom, as you did these Hebrew boys. Allow me to use my giftings to glorify your name both among your people and throughout my community. I want to be known as one who loves and serves.

Daniel 2:19–22

Then was the secret revealed unto Daniel in a night vision. Then Daniel blessed the God of heaven. Daniel answered and said, Blessed be the name of God for ever and ever: for wisdom and might are his: and he changeth the times and the seasons: he removeth kings, and setteth up kings: he giveth wisdom unto the wise, and knowledge to them that know understanding: he revealeth the deep and secret things: he knoweth what is in the darkness, and the light dwelleth with him.

King Nebuchadnezzar "dreamed dreams" that were so troubling he couldn't sleep. He summoned his magicians, sorcerers, and astrologers and required them not only to reveal the meaning of these dreams, but to tell him what the dreams had been about. The astrologers dared to say, "What the king asks is too difficult. No one can reveal it to the king except the gods, and they do not live among humans" (2:11, NIV). The king flew into a rage and ordered the execution of all the wise men in the kingdom, which included Daniel and his friends.

When the commander of the king's guard rounded up Daniel, the young man spoke "with counsel and wisdom," asking why all the wise men were being arrested. The commander explained, and Daniel went to the king, saying if he would grant him a little time, he would interpret the dream. Daniel and his friends sought the Lord for revelation. The Lord revealed it all to Daniel through a vision, and Daniel was able to tell the king both the dream and the interpretation. Daniel took none of the credit but gave all glory to God.

Whether it is for you or someone else, you should seek God for supernatural revelation. He is the revealer of secrets. There was no way Daniel could have known the answer, expect by God. You can study many things on your own—the Bible does say to study to show yourself approved. However, there are "deep and secret things" that only God can reveal. Seek his revelation.

I pray that you would reveal deep and secret things to me, Jesus, so that I might be a blessing to others. And when it happens, I will not take the credit; I will give all the glory to you.

Daniel 3:1

Nebuchadnezzar the king made an image of gold, whose height was threescore cubits, and the breadth thereof six cubits: he set it up in the plain of Dura, in the province of Babylon.

King Nebuchadnezzar has always struck me as an interesting character in the Bible. He would swing from one extreme to the other: wickedness and willful pride, to listening to Daniel and his friends and declaring the Lord to be his God, then back to wickedness and pride again. After Daniel interpreted the dream, telling Nebuchadnezzar he was the "head of gold" on the image, the king was so impressed that he declared, "Of a truth it is, that your God is a God of gods, and a Lord of kings, and a revealer of secrets, seeing thou couldest reveal this secret" (2:47). He made Daniel ruler over the whole province of Babylon and chief of the governors over all the wise men of Babylon.

But the euphoria didn't last long. In the very next chapter Nebuchadnezzar decided to erect a golden statue of himself for everyone to worship. From this we know the king had a prideful heart.

A prideful heart may acknowledge the supernatural power of God, but in the end, it will always grab acclaim and glory for itself. Paul told us not to "think of [ourselves] more highly than [we] ought, but rather think of [ourselves] with sober judgment" (Rom. 12:3, NIV). No matter how much favor the Lord places on our life, we should recognize that he is everything and we are nothing but willing vessels in his hands.

God, keep me from having a prideful heart. Though you may place favor upon me, help me not to think of myself more highly than I ought, but to think about myself with sober judgment.

Daniel 3:16–18

Shadrach, Meshach, and Abednego, answered and said to the king, O Nebuchadnezzar, we are not careful to answer thee in this matter. If it be so, our God whom we serve is able to deliver us from the burning fiery furnace, and he will deliver us out of thine hand, O king. But if not, be it known unto thee, O king, that we will not serve thy gods, nor worship the golden image which thou hast set up.

We now return to Shadrach, Meshach, and Abednego. The king had appointed them governors over the affairs of the province of Babylon (2:49). But once the king decided that everyone had to worship his image, it didn't make any difference what position a man held in the kingdom; he still had to bow.

Shadrach, Meshach, and Abednego refused to bow. They knew their God could save them from the fiery furnace, but if he didn't, they still were determined not to bow. We know this disclaimer didn't show a lack of faith because they declared that God *was able* to deliver them, but if he didn't, they still were going to serve him. That's the type of faith God likes. And God, of course, did save them from the fiery furnace and proved to a nation that he alone is God—all because of their faith.

Lord, whenever I am given the choice, I will not forsake my identity in you. I will not bow to the things of this world. I will speak faith in the middle of this test. And through it all, I will consistently choose to serve you.

Daniel 4:27–31
Wherefore, O king, let my counsel be acceptable unto thee, and break off thy sins by righteousness, and thine iniquities by shewing mercy to the poor; if it may be a lengthening of thy tranquillity. All this came upon the king Nebuchadnezzar. At the end of twelve months he walked in the palace of the kingdom of Babylon. The king spake, and said, Is not this great Babylon, that I have built for the house of the kingdom by the might of my power, and for the honour of my majesty? While the word was in the king's mouth, there fell a voice from heaven, saying, O

king Nebuchadnezzar, to thee it is spoken; The kingdom is departed from thee.

We once again see the fickleness of Nebuchadnezzar's mood swings and the crescendo of his pride. As chapter 4 opens, Nebuchadnezzar is sending a grandiose message to all the people of every race and language throughout the realm, extoling Daniel's God for revealing the meaning of another of his dreams.

In this dream the king saw a majestic tree with beautiful leaves. An angelic being came and commanded that the tree be cut down and the stump bound with iron and bronze. The angel announced that the man represented by this tree would lose his sanity and live outdoors like a wild animal for "seven times," meaning seven years.

Daniel was at first afraid to reveal the interpretation of the dream because the king's reactions were so notoriously unpredictable. But the king assured him that he really wanted to know the meaning. Daniel then revealed the dream and its interpretation, concluding, "King Nebuchadnezzar, please accept my advice. Stop sinning and do what is right. Break from your past and be merciful to the poor. Perhaps then you will continue to prosper" (v. 27, NLT).

Sadly, Nebuchadnezzar did not take Daniel's words to heart. One year later, as he strolled around the flat roof of the royal palace, he boasted, "Look at this great city of Babylon! By my own mighty power I have built this beautiful city as my royal residence to display my majestic splendor" (v. 30, NLT).

The city was indeed beautiful. There were the Hanging Gardens, considered to be one of the seven wonders of the world, magnificent temples, and the city walls were so wide that two four-horse chariots could be ridden side by side. Millions of bricks constituted the buildings in Babylon, and thousands of those bricks were stamped with boastful inscriptions about Nebuchadnezzar (*Zondervan Bible Commentary*).

While the prideful words were still rolling off the king's tongue, a clarion voice sounded from Heaven: "O king Nebuchadnezzar, to thee it is spoken; The kingdom is departed from thee!" And the dream was fulfilled in that same hour. For seven years the king lived in the fields with wild animals and ate grass like a cow; his hair grew as long as eagles' feathers, and his nails were like birds' claws.

When the set time was up, the king's sanity returned and his royal position was reinstated with even greater honor than before. The chapter ends with the king once again extoling the God of Heaven, and ending with these words: "All his acts are just and true, and he is able to humble the proud" (v. 37, NLT).

Beware of pride. You may be able to live on your own greatness for some time, but there will come a day, whether in this life or the next, when God will strip everything away. Both Peter and James addressed this subject, alluding to Proverbs 3:34: "He giveth grace unto the lowly." James said God resists the proud but gives grace to the humble (Jas. 4:6). Peter added, "Humble yourselves therefore under the mighty hand of God, that he may exalt you in due time" (1 Pet. 5:6).

You would suffer much less trauma and pain if you would lay pride on the altar—because the greatest hindrance of being useful to God is pride, and the greatest asset of being used by God is humility.

When you give all of yourself to him, he gives grace and blessing, and you will be useful to the kingdom.

Cleanse me of pride, Jesus. I kneel in humble submission before you. Without you I am nothing, but with you I can do all things. Use me as you see fit, and I will give you all the glory.

Daniel 6:3–4
Then this Daniel was preferred above the presidents and princes, because an excellent spirit was in him; and the king thought to set him over the whole realm.
Then the presidents and princes sought to find occasion against Daniel concerning the kingdom; but they could find none occasion nor fault; forasmuch as he was faithful, neither was there any error or fault found in him.

This is the type of man or woman we should aspire to be—a person with an excellent spirit. "Excellent" means extraordinary or extremely good. Daniel not only possessed an excellent spirit (upright, upbeat attitude), but his extraordinary qualities gave him the ability to excel in his job. His character was good, and he did all things well. And no one could find any fault in him.

First Timothy 3:7 (ESV) says a Christian should be "well thought of by outsiders." Proverbs 22:1 (ESV) says, "A good name is to be chosen rather than great riches, and favor is better than silver or gold." We should strive to live in such a way that even the world can recognize the excellent spirit within us.

Lord, fill me with an excellent spirit. Help me to model good character before others. Let me be faithful and true in all things—on the job, with my family, with my church, and with you.

Daniel 6:10
Now when Daniel knew that the writing was signed, he went into his house; and his windows being open in his chamber toward Jerusalem, he kneeled upon his knees three times a day, and prayed, and gave thanks before his God, as he did aforetime.

The enemy will attack anyone with an excellent spirit. He will tell lies about you. He will turn your good to evil. This is exactly what happened to Daniel. His enemies knew they couldn't catch him doing anything bad, so they conspired to make Daniel's prayers illegal. They tricked King Darius into signing a decree stating anyone who prayed to another God besides the king was breaking the law. Daniel had a decision to make.

When faced with this setback, Daniel did not change his habit of daily prayer. "As he had always done" (ESV), he went into an upstairs room three times a day, knelt down by an open window facing toward Jerusalem, and prayed. He obviously was praying aloud because the conspirators that were spying on him could hear him asking God for help. Then they knew Daniel had no intention of forsaking his God.

When the conspirators told the king, he was deeply troubled and tried to think of a way to save Daniel from the lions' den. But the conspirators demanded that the law be enforced. Right before Daniel was thrown into the lions' den, the king said to him, "May your God, whom you serve so faithfully, rescue you" (6:16, ESV).

If you get in trouble because you serve God, don't worry. Peter wrote, "If you suffer for doing good and endure it patiently, God is pleased with you" (1 Pet. 2:20, ESV). The world will see that your life is the best life.

In the end, Daniel was saved, the conspirators were cast into the lions' den, and all the people of the realm were commanded to praise the God of Daniel.

Lord, give me the faith of Daniel to pray boldly, despite my situation. I will pray publicly without fear.

Daniel 9:3–6
And I set my face unto the Lord God, to seek by prayer and supplications, with fasting, and sackcloth, and ashes: and I prayed unto the Lord my God, and made my confession, and said, O Lord, the great and dreadful God, keeping the covenant and mercy to them that love him, and to them that keep his commandments; we have sinned, and have committed iniquity, and have done wickedly, and have rebelled, even by departing from thy precepts and from thy judgments: neither have we hearkened unto

thy servants the prophets, which spake in thy name to our kings, our princes, and our fathers, and to all the people of the land.

In chapters 7 and 8, Daniel was given visions and revelations of the end time. Since many books have been written about these visions, I'm not going to go into them in any depth. Instead, I'm going to focus on Daniel's intercessory prayer.

After seeing all of these end-time prophecies, Daniel set his face, prayed, and fasted. He realized that the seventy-year period of Judah's exile as prophesied in Jeremiah 25:22–12 was soon approaching its end.

"Addressing God as Israel's faithful covenant Lord, Daniel confessed the nation's sinful and rebellious condition and acknowledged that they had justly suffered the covenant curses threatened by Moses. He then asked God to forgive the nation's sins and once again look with favor on desolate Jerusalem" (*Holman Bible Handbook*).

If God gives you revelation or prophecy of the end time, it is not just for you to know. God gave you the revelation for a reason. Daniel demonstrated this reason, as his first response was to repent on behalf of his people. Prophecy should bring repentance in knowing that God is coming back soon for his church.

Lord, when you reveal prophecy to me, let it drive me and others to repent before you. I want to be ready for your coming, Jesus.

Daniel 9:21–22

Yea, whiles I was speaking in prayer, even the man Gabriel, whom I had seen in the vision at the beginning, being caused to fly swiftly, touched me about the time of the evening oblation. And he informed me, and talked with me, and said, O Daniel, I am now come forth to give thee skill and understanding.

Daniel had been fasting and praying for twenty-one days—and when the answer came, it was so abrupt and unexpected that it left Daniel trembling. We often can get so caught up in our prayers that we forget to look for the answer. Expect an answer from the Lord! Expect him to give you understanding on the matter you are praying about. He can answer even while you are still praying.

Lord, if it's your will, I pray that you will answer my prayer swiftly. And help me to recognize the answer is from you.

Daniel 10:12–14
Then said he unto me, Fear not, Daniel: for from the first day that thou didst set thine heart to understand, and to chasten thyself before thy God, thy words were heard, and I am come for thy words. But the prince of the kingdom of Persia withstood me one and twenty days: but, lo, Michael, one of the chief princes, came to help me; and I remained there with the kings of Persia. Now I am come to make thee understand what shall befall thy people in the latter days: for yet the vision is for many days.

Evangelist Josh Herring once told me that "fasting is the quickest way into the spirit world." I have found this to be true.

Holman Illustrated Bible Dictionary estimates Daniel's age to be approaching one hundred during the reign of Darius I (511–486 BC) when he went on a twenty-one-day fast. To me this means he had a hunger to go deeper in the Lord than he had ever gone, rather than just relying on the consecration of his youth.

Second, the spirit world was activated as soon as Daniel started fasting and praying. The angel told him his prayer had been heard from day one, but he was hindered by a battle raging in the spirit world. The prince of the kingdom of Persia, an evil spirit, had withstood the angel for three weeks, until Michael, an archangel, came and fought against the evil spirit. This is an example of the war that rages in the spirit world when you begin to fast and pray.

Therefore, don't give up! It may not feel like anything is happening on day one. You may even be three days into a fast and still have not received an answer. You never know what kind of war is being fought, so keep praying and fasting. God will be victorious and will give you an answer.

Lord, give me the strength to continue praying and fasting even if it feels like you are not responding. Help me to understand that a war is being fought in the spirit world and that you will reveal your will at the right time. In Jesus' name.

Daniel 12:10
Many shall be purified, and made white, and tried; but the wicked shall do wickedly: and none of the wicked shall understand; but the wise shall understand.

The prophecies and visions we hear about regarding the end time can be confusing. However, with the help of godly teachers, pastors, and revelation, we can know the signs of the times. Pray that you will be purified before the end. Pray for understanding.

Lord, help me to be as the wise who understand prophecies and visions of the end time. Purify me so I can be ready for your coming, Jesus.

HOSEA

Hosea 1:2–3

The beginning of the word of the LORD by Hosea. And the LORD said to Hosea, Go, take unto thee a wife of whoredoms and children of whoredoms: for the land hath committed great whoredom, departing from the LORD. So he went and took Gomer the daughter of Diblaim; which conceived, and bare him a son.

Hosea's twenty-five-year ministry to the northern kingdom of Israel began during the last days of the reign of Jeroboam II and outlasted the reign of Hoshea, the last king of Israel before the Assyrian invasion. It is interesting that Hosea, the prophet's name (meaning "Yahweh is Salvation" or literally, "cause to be saved"), is the same Hebrew name as Oshea, which Moses changed to Joshua (Num. 13:16), and Hoshea, the king's name (II Kings 17:1). In the ESV, "Hoshea" was used as a verb by Abigail when she brought food to David and his men after her husband Nabal refused to help. She said, "Because the Lord has restrained you

[David] from bloodguilt and from *saving* with your own hand . . ." (1 Sam. 25:26, emphasis added).[2]

Hosea addressed the core issue of the Minor Prophets: Did Jehovah still love his people and have a purpose for them in spite of their sin and idolatry? As we will see, the Lord chose to dramatize the answer by telling Hosea to do something crazy: marry a prostitute. Why would God tell a holy prophet to do something so inappropriate?

We live in the age of the new covenant, which stresses that the Lord's commands should be obeyed because we love him. Loving submission is key. But what if God asks you to do something that sounds crazy? Should you just go ahead and do it without stopping to consider? Here's the safest way to know if you truly heard the Lord's voice: If it is something contrary to the word of God and the spiritual authority in your life (pastor, church leader, etc.) then the voice you heard was not God's voice.

---

[2] Jeff A. Benner, "Hosea" ancient-hebrew.org/names/Hosea.htm.

When Hosea heard the voice telling him to marry a prostitute, he knew it definitely was God's voice, because God told him point-blank that he was using the prophet's life to parallel the rocky relationship between God and Israel. So Hosea obeyed and chose a wife who was unfaithful as a sign of the unfaithfulness of Israel to their God.

This also should be a sign to us. When we are unfaithful to God, we are acting like a woman who is unfaithful to her husband. Yet, despite his wife's unfaithfulness, Hosea's love for Gomer remained steadfast throughout the book. Above all else we should avoid a Gomer-like attitude or spirit and instead remain a part of the faithful bride of Christ.

Jesus, I want to be faithful to you. I will continue to spend time in relationship with you daily. I will go to church, pray, study your word, and seek your face in all things. I want to be a part of the faithful bride of Christ.

Hosea 2:14

Therefore, behold, I will allure her, and bring her into the wilderness, and speak comfortably unto her.

Through Hosea, the Lord spoke harshly to Israel: "You are no longer my wife, and I am no longer your husband!" Israel's prolonged pursuit of other gods had finally come to a head; God was finally going to make good on his warnings to force them out of their beautiful, fertile land and send them as captives into Assyria.

But the Lord's anger does not last forever, especially when it concerns his people. He promised that after Israel had been sufficiently punished, he would win them back again, return them to their land, and speak tenderly to them. He said, "I will make you my wife forever, showing you righteousness and justice, unfailing love and compassion. I will be faithful to you and make you mine, and you will finally know me as the LORD" (2:19–20, NLT).

Though God may chastise us for our wrongs, it won't be long before he assures us that he is a loving husband. He will rescue us away from the noise, the trouble, and the hurt, and give us some alone time with him. He will speak tenderly to us, even though we've been unfaithful. That is who God is—a loving husband.

God, thank you for your faithfulness to me even though I don't deserve it. Take me to a place alone with you so you can help me mend my ways. Speak comfort to me, and I will repent and turn back to your never-ending love.

Hosea 4:6–7
My people are destroyed for lack of knowledge: because thou hast rejected knowledge, I will also reject thee, that thou shalt be no priest to me: seeing thou hast forgotten the law of thy God, I will also forget thy children. As they were increased, so they sinned against me: therefore will I change their glory into shame.

The Lord said the root cause of the people's destruction was lack of knowledge. His repeated indictments against them for idolatry and unfaithfulness led to the understanding that this lack of knowledge wasn't just plain ignorance; they were ignorant of the most important thing—knowledge of God. To know God is to have a relationship with him. Peter wrote, "Grow in grace, and in the knowledge of our Lord and Saviour Jesus Christ" (2 Pet. 3:18).

Why did God's people know more about Baal worship and golden-calf worship than they knew about Jehovah? Because they were unfaithful to their covenant with the Lord and avoided any kind of meaningful relationship with him.

A short historical review explains, in part, how this came about: When the northern kingdom of Israel split off from the southern kingdom of Judah, Jeroboam, the first king of Israel, in order to keep his kingdom politically and religiously separate, did two strategic things: (1) He instituted worship of the Lord at the altars of two golden calves, one in Dan (to the north, almost on the border with Syria) and the other in Bethel (to the south, almost on the border with Judah). (2) He "cast off" the priests and Levites (2 Chron. 11:13–14) and instead ordained priests of every class of people who were not of the tribe of Levi.

Consequently, there was a mass migration to Judah and Jerusalem of priests, Levites, and tribal people who had "set their hearts to seek the Lord God of Israel."

Malachi wrote, "The words of the priest's lips should preserve knowledge of God, and the people should go to him for instruction." If the priests throughout Israel's history were teaching the people, it certainly wasn't about the pure law of the Lord; it was about pagan-style worship. All but three of Israel's kings "did evil in the sight of Lord" by following after the sins of Jeroboam—the king who had set up the golden calves.

The other main deity was Baal, introduced during the reign of Ahab. Baal was often represented in the form of a large bull or ram, and these sculptures were erected in shrines and temples. Baal continued to be worshiped during the reigns of the two kings who succeeded Ahab, until Jehu destroyed the house of Ahab and the Baal worshipers. Jehu, however, did not destroy calf worship, and it continued until Israel fell.

The Lord said, "The children of Israel walked in all the sins of Jeroboam which he did; they departed not from them; until the LORD removed Israel out of his sight, as he had said by all his servants the prophets. So was Israel carried away out of their own land to Assyria" (2 Kings 17:22–23). This tragedy happened in 722 BC.

Lord, I want to grow in grace and knowledge of you so that I may have a meaningful relationship with you, my Lord and Savior Jesus Christ. I will study your word and listen to the teaching of the man of God so that knowledge of you will fill my life. Amen.

Hosea 6:1–2
Come, and let us return unto the LORD: for he hath torn, and he will heal us; he hath smitten, and he will bind us up. After two days will he revive us: in the third day he will raise us up, and we shall live in his sight.

One of the amazing things to know about God is that he is our heavenly Father. What does a good father do when his children misbehave? He corrects them. And the most effective correction (punishment) is meted out with love, not anger. Although the correction—in whatever form—may hurt, it causes children to correct their ways.

Hebrews 12:6 (NLT) says, "For the LORD disciplines those he loves, and he punishes each one he accepts as his child." The writer of Hebrews was quoting Proverbs 3:11–12 (NLT) when he wrote, "My child, don't reject the LORD's discipline, and don't be upset when he corrects you."

Are you being chastised? Punished? Corrected? Don't become resentful or angry at God because the correction is issuing out of a heart full of fatherly love, compassion, mercy, and goodness. If God didn't care about the sins you commit or how your life will end, he would let you do anything you want, go anywhere you want, have any kind of attitude you want, say anything you want (you get the picture) without lifting a finger to set you back on the right path.

Therefore, we see that his correction is an act of love. We can see it as a sure sign that he accepts us as his child and wants to have a close relationship with us. We can trust in his correction, knowing it is for our good and it will help us get back on the right path.

Do you feel like he has torn you to pieces? It won't be long before he will come and put you back together again. Are you smarting from the injuries he has inflicted? He will soon come and bandage your wounds. Read Hosea 6:2 (NLT) as a personal message to you: "In just a short time God will come and restore [me] so that [I] may live in his presence."

Lord, I realize you are correcting me for the wrongs I have committed. Thank you for the correction, Lord, because it is an affirmation that you love me, that you consider me your child, and that you want to be in close relationship with me. I repent before you so that I may be restored and once again live in your presence. Amen.

Hosea 8:3
Israel hath cast off the thing that is good: the enemy shall pursue him.

When Israel saw the Assyrian horde descending on them like a bird of prey, they cried out to God in terror. But by then it was too late. They had already cast off the thing that was good. They had broken their covenant with God and rebelled against God's law. It was a chilling pronouncement.

Hosea wrote, "This calf you worship, O Israel, was crafted by your own hands! It is not God! Therefore, it must be smashed to bits" (v. 6, NLT).

Like David, I'm asking you not to cast me away from your presence, Lord. Don't take your Holy Spirit from me. Wash me from my iniquity and cleanse me from my sin. Restore unto me the joy of your salvation, and uphold me with your free Spirit.

Let me never cast you out of my life, Lord, because you are the best thing that has ever happened to me. I pray you will be Lord of my life and Lord of my family's lives. In Jesus' name.

Hosea 10:2

Their heart is divided; now shall they be found faulty: he shall break down their altars, he shall spoil their images.

Jeremiah wrote, "The heart is deceitful above all things, and desperately wicked: who can know it? I the LORD search the heart, I try the reins, even to give every man according to his ways, and according to the fruit of his doings" (Jer. 17:9–10).

Israel had a deceitful heart. At times they went through the motions of worshiping the Lord, and in times of distress they cried out to him. But then they would dishonor him by worshiping pagan gods.

A divided heart is no good. Gomer was a real-life representation of Israel's divided heart. Hosea married her knowing full well she would be unfaithful. The names of Gomer's three children reflect this: (1) Their firstborn son was named Jezreel ("Scattered"). Israel would soon be scattered by a whirlwind. (2) The second child was a daughter named Lo-Ruhamah ("No Mercy"). No matter how desperately Israel cried, it was now too late. God would show no mercy. (3)

Gomer's third child, another boy, was named Lo-Ammi ("Not My People"). The Lord was disowning his people, Israel.

You can't achieve any kind of meaningful relationship with God with a divided heart. You must give *all* to him.

Lord, I will not have a divided heart. I will love you with all my heart, soul, mind, and strength. I'm giving myself to you.

Hosea 10:12
Sow to yourselves in righteousness, reap in mercy; break up your fallow ground: for it is time to seek the Lord, till he come and rain righteousness upon you.

Through the prophets, Israel had been entreated to "plant good seeds of righteousness" so they could reap a crop of love. God had urged, "Plow up the hard ground of your hearts, for now is the time to seek the Lord, that he may come and shower righteousness on you" (Hos. 10:12, NLT). But as we have seen, they didn't listen. Their hearts were like fallow fields—barren, hard packed, overgrown with weeds.

How does a person plant seeds of righteousness in his or her heart? First, just as a farmer will plow and harrow and fertilize and plant, you must work hard in order to reap a crop of righteousness. It takes time and effort. It takes spiritual disciplines: studying the word of God and prayer. It takes loving others as yourself, doing good, and being a good example for believers and non-believers alike. What will be your reward for all of your labor? Mercy and righteousness.

God, I will sow righteous seeds in my life. I will work hard to become a righteous person. Show me your mercy in return. In Jesus' name.

Hosea 14:1–4 (NLT)
Return, O Israel, to the LORD your God, for your sins have brought you down. Bring your confessions, and return to the LORD. Say to him, "Forgive all our sins and graciously receive us, so that we may offer you our praises. Assyria cannot save us, nor can our

warhorses. Never again will we say to the idols we have made, "You are our gods." No, in you alone do the orphans find mercy. The Lord says, "Then I will heal you of your faithlessness; my love will know no bounds, for my anger will be gone forever."

This is one of the most reassuring and comforting passages in the word of God. It tells you that you can never stray so far from the Lord that your relationship with him cannot be restored—if you will repent and turn back to him.

The Lord depicted this through the life of Hosea and Gomer. Hosea's love for his faithless wife never wavered. Even though she had children by other men and had become enslaved by sin, Hosea went looking for her and redeemed her from slavery. He brought her back to his house to love her and cherish her as his wife. Hosea wrote in 3:4 (NLT), "But afterward the people will return and devote themselves to the Lord their God . . . In the last days they will tremble in awe of the Lord and of his goodness."

Lord, thank you for keeping your eye on me even as I was straying far from you. Thank you for caring enough to hear me when my soul cried out to you. Thank you for coming to my rescue and for forgiving me and restoring me to your household. In Jesus' name, amen.

JOEL
Joel 1:2–3

Hear this, ye old men, and give ear, all ye inhabitants of the land. Hath this been in your days, or even in the days of your fathers? Tell ye your children of it, and let your children tell their children, and their children another generation.

So few details are known about the prophet Joel that it is difficult to pinpoint the dates of his ministry. However, many Bible scholars place him in late seventh century BC, during the reign of King Joash of Judah. The Apostolic Study Bible says that numerous references within the book point to an author based in Jerusalem.

The Old Testament contains many admonitions that parents should teach their children about the Lord, his mighty acts, and his faithfulness. Moses told them to talk about God throughout the day and at bedtime (Deut. 11:19). David urged parents to teach their children and grandchildren about the Lord (Ps. 34:11; 145:4). Asaph, in his brief account of Israel's history, counseled parents to show to generations to come the praises of the Lord (Ps. 78:4–6).

Joel also stressed the importance of teaching one's children about the Lord. In essence, he said, "What I'm about to say isn't just for you; it's also for the generations to come. Don't expect your children to absorb spiritual truths through some kind of mysterious osmosis. Your children and the generations to come need to hear it from you!"

The gospel works by passing it down from one generation to the next. Every blessing, every prophecy, every good word, and every victory should be taught and celebrated. Make this a commitment: "Lord, I will not let what I know about you and your word die with me; I will pass it on to the next generation."

Lord, I will pass your gospel to the next generation. I will teach them your word, recount your victories, and testify of your blessings.

Joel 1:12–14

The vine is dried up, and the fig tree languisheth; the pomegranate tree, the palm tree also, and the apple tree, even all the trees of the field, are withered: because joy is withered away from the sons of men.

Gird yourselves, and lament, ye priests: howl, ye ministers of the altar: come, lie all night in sackcloth, ye ministers of my God: for the meat offering and the drink offering is withholden from the house of your God. Sanctify ye a fast, call a solemn assembly, gather the elders and all the inhabitants of the land into the house of the LORD your God, and cry unto the LORD.

The southern kingdom of Judah was in a bad state. Their sin and godlessness had withered away their joy, just as the drought was withering away their pastures and crops. Their fair land had once been "as the garden of Eden before them" (2:3), but, in addition to the drought, a voracious army of locusts had invaded and devoured every green thing.

Why did God allow such devastation to fall on his people? Joel was hoping the tragedy would draw them back to God. They were to gather the people together, call for a fast, and lament the pain and suffering. They were to cry out to God in their sorrow.

God, I cry out to you in my sorrow. I will lament, repent, fast, and pray to you.

Joel 2:12–13
Therefore also now, saith the LORD, turn ye even to me with all your heart, and with fasting, and with weeping, and with mourning: and rend your heart, and not your garments, and turn unto the LORD your God: for he is gracious and merciful, slow to anger, and of great kindness, and repenteth him of the evil.

What a blessed passage! In our hopelessness we can turn to him with the assurance that he will mend our broken heart. The NLT says, "Return to the LORD your God, for he is merciful and compassionate, slow to get angry and filled with unfailing love. He is eager to relent and not punish" (v. 13). That is the God we serve.

God, I come before you with fasting and prayer. Mend me, Jesus. Mend my heart with your grace, mercy, patience, and kindness.

Joel 2:21
Fear not, O land; be glad and rejoice: for the Lord will do great things.

What is the result of our fasting and crying out to God? He will do great things!

Lord, do great things in and around my life!

Joel 2:23–27
Be glad then, ye children of Zion, and rejoice in the Lord your God: for he hath given you the former rain moderately, and he will cause to come down for you the rain, the former rain, and the latter rain in the first month. And the floors shall be full of wheat, and the vats shall overflow with wine and oil. And I will restore to you the years that the locust hath eaten, the cankerworm, and the caterpiller, and the palmerworm, my great army which I sent among you.

And ye shall eat in plenty, and be satisfied, and praise the name of the LORD your God, that hath dealt wondrously with you: and my people shall never be ashamed. And ye shall know that I am in the midst of Israel, and that I am the LORD your God, and none else: and my people shall never be ashamed.

The prophecies and blessings in Joel 2 are incredible! First, this passage says God will give the former rain and the latter rain in the first month. That means the blessings you received in the beginning will be combined with the blessings you will receive at the end. It is a blessing of multiplication, and it's going to happen quickly!

Not only will your time of dryness and spiritual drought end, the Lord will restore "all the years that the locust hath eaten." To Judah, this meant their first crop after the drought would be so bountiful that it would make up for the two or three crops they had lost during the famine. All the increase, both financial and spiritual, that you thought you had lost from the hurt and pain of the Lord's chastisement, he will restore.

You will no longer have to wonder if God has forgotten about you or if he cares what you're going through. There will be no doubt in your mind that God is for you. And you will never be ashamed.

God, I rejoice in the showers of blessings and bask in the sunlight of your presence! Thank you for restoring the things that I thought were gone forever. Thank you for the assurance that you are for me and with me. You are the best!

Joel 2:28–32

And it shall come to pass afterward, that I will pour out my spirit upon all flesh; and your sons and your daughters shall prophesy, your old men shall dream dreams, your young men shall see visions: and also upon the servants and upon the handmaids in those days will I pour out my spirit. And I will shew wonders in the heavens and in the earth, blood, and fire, and pillars of smoke. The sun shall be turned into darkness, and the moon into blood, before the great and terrible day of the LORD come. And it shall come to pass, that whosoever shall call on the name of the LORD shall be delivered: for in mount Zion and in Jerusalem shall be deliverance, as the LORD hath said, and in the remnant whom the LORD shall call.

The apostle Peter quoted this passage during his sermon on the Day of Pentecost, saying, "This is that which was spoken by the prophet Joel" (Acts 1:16). Centuries before the actual event, Joel had prophesied the outpouring of the Holy Spirit. Peter declared, "The promise is unto you, and to your children, and to all that are afar off, even as many as the Lord our God shall call" (Acts 2:39).

Everybody—all flesh—is eligible to receive the Spirit of God! If you've been questioning whether or not the Holy Spirit is for you, this is your proof; it is for all flesh. Don't let this wonderful prophecy go unfulfilled in your life. Receive the Spirit that God is waiting to give you. Call on the name of Jesus and believe.

God, I believe the prophecy of your spiritual outpouring. I believe the promise is for me, as Peter

preached on the Day of Pentecost. Fill me with your Spirit, Jesus!

Joel 3:13–14

Put ye in the sickle, for the harvest is ripe: come, get you down; for the press is full, the fats overflow; for their wickedness is great. Multitudes, multitudes in the valley of decision: for the day of the LORD is near in the valley of decision.

A sickle is a primitive tool used to reap the harvest. This particular "harvest" prefigures Armageddon, where God will judge the nations in the "valley of decision." But there is hope for God's people. The end of the chapter assures them that God will make all things right. He will bless those who repent and reward them with righteousness.

But there is another great harvest in this end time. Jesus mentioned it in John 4:35: "Behold, I say unto you, Lift up your eyes, and look on the fields; for they are white already to harvest." This harvest is souls who are "ripe"—ready to give their hearts to God. Since so many are ready, start reaching out for them.

Start teaching Bible studies. Start inviting them to church. Start having conversations about God. Lead people to that decision. Because there are multitudes waiting in the fields, ready to make that choice to receive the Spirit of God.

Lord, I will work in the field to reap your harvest. Lead me to people who are ready to receive you and who will decide to serve you. In Jesus' name.

AMOS

Amos 3:3

Can two walk together, except they be agreed?

Amos is an interesting Bible character because, although he had a brief prophetic ministry, he said, "I'm not a professional prophet, and I was never trained to be one. I'm just a shepherd, and I take care of sycamore-fig trees. But the LORD called me away from my flock and told me, 'Go and prophesy to my people in Israel'" (7:14–15, NLT). Amos's foray into Israel also is interesting since Amos lived in Tekoa, a village located about twelve miles south of Jerusalem in Judean territory.

Amos lived and prophesied during a time of great prosperity and peace in both Israel (under King Jeroboam II) and Judah (under King Uzziah). God's people usually equated peace and prosperity as a sign of God's blessing and favor; however, the rich were getting richer and exploiting the poor. Israel's religion was corrupt; they were going through the motions of worshiping the Lord at the altars of the golden calves in Dan and Bethel.

The message from the Lord burned so fiercely inside of Amos that he left his flocks and journeyed across the border into Israel to Bethel, where he prophesied.

In the middle of his rebukes against empty religion and ill-gotten prosperity, Amos asked this question: "Can two walk together in unity if they don't agree?"

You must realize that if you are not agreeing with the things of God by following his commandments, you are not walking with him. It doesn't matter how much you pray or go to church or how spiritual you think you are; you are not in unity with God if your life is not in alignment with the word of God. In order to walk with God, you must pursue the same things Jesus pursued. Make it your aim to walk with God.

God, I want to be in unity and agreement with you. Help me to pursue what you think is right and to follow your commandments.

Amos 4:12

Therefore thus will I do unto thee, O Israel: and because I will do this unto thee, prepare to meet thy God, O Israel.

The Apostolic Study Bible says, "Here [in vv. 4:11–12] Amos used a double comparison. God destroyed some in Israel after the manner of Sodom, and he rescued some after the manner of Lot's rescue. As a whole, Israel had reenacted the narratives of both the Sodomites and those rescued from Sodom." Now Israel must face the God they had covenanted with at the foot of Mount Sinai, whose covenant they had violated. They heard this terrifying message: "Prepare to meet thy God, O Israel!"

There are two ways to meet our God. One, flaunt our sin, neglect his word, practice a pretense of religion, and refuse to heed the warnings the Lord sends until his patience is gone and he sends judgment. Two, we approach his throne with humble, repentant hearts, lay ourselves on the altar as a living sacrifice, and let him restore us to true relationship with him.

Desire the second way of meeting God. Come to him, and he will accept you with love.

God, I don't want to try your patience like Israel did. I want to serve you unreservedly with my whole heart. Search my heart, and renew in me a right spirit. I want my meeting with you to be one of joy and rejoicing, not fear and regret.

Amos 5:4
*For thus saith the L*ORD *unto the house of Israel, Seek ye me, and ye shall live.*

Despite all of the horrible sins Israel had committed, their path to redemption was simple—seek God. The path to redemption is still simple. We must simply seek him. And when we seek him with our whole heart, we will find him because he is merciful.

Lord, drive me to seek you when I have been unfaithful. I want to live in your presence.

OBADIAH

Obadiah 1:3–4

The pride of thine heart hath deceived thee, thou that dwellest in the clefts of the rock, whose habitation is high; that saith in his heart, Who shall bring me down to the ground? Though thou exalt thyself as the eagle, and though thou set thy nest among the stars, thence will I bring thee down, saith the Lord.

Nothing is known about Obadiah except that his name means "servant or worshiper of Jehovah." Obadiah's book is the shortest in the Bible, but his message had great impact. It was an indictment against Edom, the country southeast of Judah below the Dead Sea.

Animosity had existed between Israel and Edom for centuries. Edomites were descendants of Esau, Jacob's twin brother. Esau was profane and careless, and his descendants inherited those traits. The story of the two brothers in Genesis is one of deception on Jacob's part and murderous intent on Esau's part.

Then, during the Exodus when Israel needed to pass through Edom on their way to the Promised Land, Edom flatly refused passage. Even worse, during the destruction of Jerusalem, the Edomites eagerly helped the Babylonians in the sacking of Jerusalem and turned over the Jews who were trying to flee. Then, in the aftermath of the deportation when Judah's population was depleted, Edom expanded westward and annexed the southern region of Judean territory.

Edomites were proud. They inhabited the territory in the Mountains of Seir, and their central city was Petra. They bragged about the city's natural defenses; they thought they were unconquerable. They never dreamed God Almighty would refute their claims: "Thou that dwellest in the cleft of the rock . . . I will bring thee down . . . thou shalt be cut off forever." Sure enough, Edomites disappeared from history after the destruction of Jerusalem in AD 70.

The Lord does not take pride lightly. Proverbs 6:16–17 tells us that God hates pride. Edomites had a "proud look," indicating they looked down on other people while overestimating their own importance. They felt they were soaring with the eagles.

Pride is the fuel for soaring with the eagles, but those flights are only vain, empty gusts of imagination. The Edomites thought they were living high, but they eventually fell.

Isaiah indicated we cannot soar like the eagles without waiting upon God. Wait until God exalts you and takes you to high places.

Lord, I pray against empty pride in my life. I pray that you would be the one to exalt me and not my own pride.

Obadiah 1:17
But upon mount Zion shall be deliverance, and there shall be holiness; and the house of Jacob shall possess their possessions.

Verse 17 begins to list the blessings awaiting Judah and Israel in the future. The southern and northern kingdoms will one day be reunited, and the house of Edom will be destroyed. The restoration of Judah and Israel will involve an expansion of their territory. The Lord will be the ruler of this reunited kingdom.

The writer of Hebrews said, "Ye are come unto mount Zion, and unto the city of the living God, the heavenly Jerusalem, and to an innumerable company of angels" (Heb. 12:22). Salvation and deliverance are still available on mount Zion, the church. Seek the Lord's holiness, and he will deliver you.

Lord, I need deliverance; therefore, I will seek your face and your holiness. I want to dwell with you on mount Zion.

JONAH

Jonah 1:1–3

Now the word of the Lord came unto Jonah the son of Amittai, saying, Arise, go to Nineveh, that great city, and cry against it; for their wickedness is come up before me. But Jonah rose up to flee unto Tarshish from the presence of the Lord, and went down to Joppa; and he found a ship going to Tarshish: so he paid the fare thereof, and went down into it, to go with them unto Tarshish from the presence of the Lord.

Jonah lived during the early part of Israel's golden age under Jeroboam II. At that time, Assyria was in a weakened state, which allowed for the expansion of both Israel and Judah. Jonah was a contemporary of Amos, but his mission was not domestic; it was to the foreign city of Nineveh.

Apparently, the trouble started because of Jonah's isolationism (Lockyer, *All the Men of the Bible*); he believed salvation was Israel's prerogative. In addition, Assyria's fearsome reputation turned Jonah off to the extent he didn't want them to be saved.

After the Lord's call, Jonah's journey should have gone from his home in Gath-hepher (two-and-a-half miles northeast of Nazareth) directly to the revival in Nineveh (on the west bank of the Tigris River). Instead, Jonah ran from the call of God to Joppa—a seaport in Philistine territory—and boarded a ship bound for Tarshish. Some maps of the ancient world show that Tarshish was located in Spain. Jonah couldn't get any farther away from God's call to Nineveh than that!

There was a good reason for Jonah's fear of the Assyrians. Notoriously cruel, violent, and idolatrous, they were "responsible for the harassment and exploitation Israel and Judah [had] suffered over more than a century" (*Holman Bible Handbook*). Jonah ran away from the call of God for several possible reasons: prejudice against these heathens, intimidation, or terror of standing alone with a message of judgment and destruction against a city of an estimated two hundred to six hundred thousand people. He would not be a popular guy.

Jonah's flight from the presence of God was downhill all the way: down to Joppa, down into the bottom of the ship, down into the belly of a fish, and down to the "roots of the mountains" (NIV). As soon as you start running from the call of God, your life will go into a tailspin.

Lord, I don't want to run from your calling. Give me the strength and courage and boldness to rise up and pursue your calling over my life.

Jonah 1:4–5

But the LORD sent out a great wind into the sea, and there was a mighty tempest in the sea, so that the ship was like to be broken. Then the mariners were afraid, and cried every man unto his god, and cast forth the wares that were in the ship into the sea, to lighten it of them. But Jonah was gone down into the sides of the ship; and he lay, and was fast asleep.

God didn't force Jonah to go to Nineveh; he made him want to go to Nineveh. He sent a violent tempest into Jonah's life. Fearing the ship would break apart in the boisterous winds and crashing waves, sailors began tossing cargo over the side. Where was Jonah amidst all of this turmoil? In the hold of the ship sound asleep. He had ignored the call of God, then he fell asleep.

Beware of falling asleep at the wrong time. God is not against you enjoying a good night's sleep or taking a vacation; however, if you will let him, the enemy will cause you to ignore your calling and instead settle yourself for a nice long sleep.

What is the difference between godly rest and sleeping away your calling? Godly rest refreshes you so you can pursue prayer, study of God's word, and your relationship with him. A little sleep, a little slumber at the wrong time, on the other hand, will push you down: a step down from ministry; a step down from prayer; a step down from godly relationships; a step down from faithfulness.

Godly rest balances our spiritual and natural lives; deceptive rest irradicates spiritual disciplines. Godly rest (quiet times with God) allows us to listen to his wise counsel; deceptive rest causes us to listen to our carnal nature and give in to fleshly desires. Wasting time on movies, social media, and pulling away from godly friends is not rest; it is a ploy of the enemy.

Evaluate your rest. If you find yourself ignoring spiritual leaders or cutting back on spiritual disciplines, it's time to awake out of rest and go back to work in the kingdom. You have a calling. You have a purpose. Wake up. Nineveh needs you.

Lord, help me to evaluate my rest. Don't let me be lulled to sleep by the enemy. Let me fulfill your calling on my life. Give me boldness to reach out to my Nineveh.

Jonah 1:17

Now the LORD had prepared a great fish to swallow up Jonah. And Jonah was in the belly of the fish three days and three nights.

The distraught sailors knew this fellow Jonah was to blame for their troubles because he had told them he was running from the Lord. They hurriedly climbed down into the ship's hold and shook him awake. "What should we do to you to make the sea calm down for us?" "Pick me up and throw me into the sea . . . I know that it is my fault that this great storm has come upon you" (NIV). So the sailors grabbed Jonah, threw him overboard, and immediately there was a great calm. Along came a great fish and swallowed Jonah.

It is interesting to me that this fish, which seems to be a punishment, was in fact the means of saving Jonah's life. Without the great fish God had prepared, Jonah would have drowned.

Thrown into the sea, the currents swirled around him. He spluttered and gasped as waves and breakers swept over him. He cried, "The engulfing waters threatened me, the deep surrounded me; seaweed was wrapped around my head" (2:5, 7, NIV).

For three days and night, while Jonah was languishing in the fish's belly, that fish swam eastward toward the coastline of Palestine. Jonah loathed his repulsive environment—digestive juices and partially digested food. But as time passed, he began to repent. He said, "When my life was ebbing away, I remembered you, Lord" (2:7, NIV). He vowed he would "make good" on his calling. He declared, "Salvation comes from the LORD!" (2:9, NIV).

Are you being tossed about on winds of trouble and overwhelmed by waves? Does God have you trapped in an uncomfortable situation? He may be sparing you from certain death. Recognize that storms can sometimes be God preparing a way of escape for you. Recognize the time of trouble as an opportunity to turn back to him.

Lord, thank you for preparing a way of escape from my storm. I will repent before you in the middle of my darkest trial.

Jonah 2:9–10

But I will sacrifice unto thee with the voice of thanksgiving; I will pay that that I have vowed. Salvation is of the LORD. And the LORD spake unto the fish, and it vomited out Jonah upon the dry land.

God had been waiting for Jonah's prayer of thanksgiving. No sooner had the prophet finished praying than the fish swam onto the beach and belched him up on dry land. The prophet's skin was pale and shriveled from stomach acid. His clothes were slimy. He stank. But at least he was alive. He got to his feet with renewed zeal, determined to do God's will.

Giving thanks may not feel like the right approach when you're in the middle of your darkest trial, but I encourage you to try it. God loves and deserves your praise in every situation. And as stated earlier, that trial may truly be your salvation. So give thanks.

Thank you for your salvation, Lord. Even when I'm in the worst trial of my life, I will give you thanks.

Jonah 3:1–2
And the word of the LORD came unto Jonah the second time, saying, Arise, go unto Nineveh, that great city, and preach unto it the preaching that I bid thee.

If the Lord gives you a second chance to speak his word and carry out his will, consider yourself blessed. Do not miss the opportunity this time. Be like Jonah. Arise and go to your Nineveh.

Lord, I know I ran from your calling the first time, but it will not happen again. Call me and use me, Lord. Tell me what you want me to do and I will do it. I will arise and go.

Jonah 3:5
So the people of Nineveh believed God, and proclaimed a fast, and put on sackcloth, from the greatest of them even to the least of them.

One of the greatest lessons to learn from the story of Jonah is that God will forgive even the most wicked people if they will repent.

We can tell from Jonah's actions after his preaching campaign that he really didn't expect the Ninevites to repent and was "exceedingly displeased" when they did. He found a spot where he could overlook the city to see what would happen, possibly hoping fire and brimstone would reduce the city to ashes.

Jonah was at cross-purposes with God as expressed in the following short poem titled "Coming Around":

And Jonah stalked
to his shaded seat
and waited for God
to come around
to his way of thinking.

And God is still waiting
for a host of Jonah's
to come around
to his way of loving.[3]

God forbid that we take a Jonah-like attitude. Who are we to judge who will and won't repent? Nineveh, the largest city in the world at the time, was also one of the most wicked cities, yet the Bible says they believed God and everyone repented from the greatest to the least. You never know who will respond to the message God gives you.

---

[3] T. J. Carlisle, *You! Jonah!* (Grand Rapids: 1968, p. 64); as quoted in *Old Testament Survey* 2nd ed., eds. William LaSor et al. (Grand Rapids: Eerdmans, 1996).

The next time you get that feeling to invite _____ to church or to ask _____ if they need prayer, don't ignore it or question it. You may think, *This person would never want what I have to share with them.* You may even think, *I'm not sure I want them coming to my church anyway.* You are not God. God loves everyone. Seek to be like him; don't be willing that any should perish.

Lord, when you tell me to witness to someone, I will not judge. I will simply arise and do what you say.

Jonah 4:1
But it displeased Jonah exceedingly, and he was very angry.

In the aftermath of Jonah's powerful preaching, Nineveh repented and the city was spared. This bruised Jonah's pride and made him angry. He told God, "See? This is why I went to Tarshish! I knew you were merciful and kind and slow to anger. I knew you would change your mind."

This is the greatest tragedy of the story of Jonah: the preacher was upset that people had heeded his warning.

Remember we are not the judge of who should and shouldn't be saved; we are only the messengers of the gospel. Nineveh's cruel and sordid past was not a determiner of their future.

God said to Jonah, "Nineveh has more than 120,000 people living in spiritual darkness, not to mention all the animals. Shouldn't I feel sorry for such a great city?" (4:11, NLT). The lost cannot even discern their sinful condition. We have no right to judge them when they don't even know that what they are doing is sinful. Our job is simply to do the work of God and let him be the judge.

Obviously, Jonah was a powerful preacher; his message led to an entire city being converted. One would think he would be ecstatic with the result, but instead he became angry and complained to God. He was gifted, yes. He got phenomenal results, yes. But the book ends with Jonah displaying a bad attitude. Which causes me to wonder if the people of Nineveh had a better chance than Jonah to enter God's kingdom.

Keep your attitude right. You are not above God. Remember God is sovereign and humble yourself before him.

God, purge me of every bad attitude. Build my character, not just my gifting. Never let me be angry when a soul repents. Give me your love for people.

MICAH

Micah 4:1–2

But in the last days it shall come to pass, that the mountain of the house of the LORD shall be established in the top of the mountains, and it shall be exalted above the hills; and people shall flow unto it. And many nations shall come, and say, Come, and let us go up to the mountain of the LORD, and to the house of the God of Jacob; and he will teach us of his ways, and we will walk in his paths: for the law shall go forth of Zion, and the word of the LORD from Jerusalem.

Micah, a contemporary of Isaiah, lived in the southern kingdom of Judah during the reigns of Ahaz and Hezekiah. He, like Isaiah, gave prophecies concerning the destruction of Israel. He addressed several injustices in the northern nation: the rich were cheating the poor by confiscating their land and stealing their possessions; rulers were not enforcing justice; the nation was practicing a syncretic form of religion—they still believed in Jehovah but combined worship of him with other gods; they didn't think Sabbath worship had anything to do with how they conducted their daily lives.

However, Micah also injected a message of hope: "In the last days, the LORD's house will be . . . the most important place on earth. . . . People from all over the world will stream there to worship. . . . The Lord's teaching will go out from Zion" (4:1–2, NLT).

We can claim this message of redemption for all nations.

Lord, I pray that you will redeem many people in these last days. I pray that you will teach us how to walk in your ways.

Micah 6:8

He hath shewed thee, O man, what is good; and what doth the LORD require of thee, but to do justly, and to love mercy, and to walk humbly with thy God?

The people needed to know that what was taught in the house of the Lord should be lived out in their daily lives. In this key verse, "Micah beautifully encapsulated what God wants from his people: a pure heart that serves God and serves others. . . . Their salvation came through their obedience to conditions of God's covenant" (Apostolic Study Bible). God simply wanted them to do justly, love mercy, and walk humbly with him.

Many times, doing the right thing doesn't require a lot of study or thought. It is simply obeying the word of God. If you align with his commandments, you will do the right thing.

You are required to love mercy, because you will inevitably stumble at times, and so will others. So, for your sake and for the sake of others, be merciful. When you are not doing justly, you must depend on God's mercy; when others are not doing justly, they must depend on your mercy. Be ready to extend it.

Finally, you are to walk humbly with your God. Never think you have it all figured out. This is a journey. Keep on seeking him and you will find the will of God for your life.

Lord, I will do justly, love mercy, and walk humbly with you. When others need it, I will extend mercy to them just as you extend mercy to me. Amen.

Micah 7:7–8

Therefore I will look unto the LORD; I will wait for the God of my salvation: my God will hear me. Rejoice not against me, O mine enemy: when I fall, I shall arise; when I sit in darkness, the LORD shall be a light unto me.

I love these verses because they exude faith. "I will wait, and God will hear me; when I fall, I shall arise! When I sit in darkness, the Lord shall be a light!" Learn to speak to your trouble with positivity. This isn't just a new-age method for coping; it is scriptural. So don't just think positive, speak positive!

Lord, I know this trouble won't last forever. I will wait until you rescue me. When I fall, you will help me to get back up. When darkness is all around me, you will be my light.

NAHUM

Nahum 1:7

The LORD is good, a strong hold in the day of trouble; and he knoweth them that trust in him.

Nahum prophesied about 150 years after Jonah. The messages of both of these prophets concerned the Assyrian Empire, which, at the time of Nahum, was still at the peak of its power.

The effects of Jonah's revival were long gone and Assyria was worse than ever. Its people were proud of the fact that they didn't have any more space for the bodies of their enemies. They heaped up pyramids of human heads and covered pillars with the flayed skins of their victims (Lockyer, *All the Men of the Bible*).

Amidst Nahum's message of impending destruction for Nineveh, he inserted a glimmer of hope for Judah. Nahum 1:9 indicates that although Assyrians had conquered the northern kingdom of Israel, the Lord would not allow them to molest Judah. Instead, Nineveh itself would come to an "utter end."

The language in 1:2–8 seems to recall other biblical passages; for example, "The LORD is good" (Ps. 34:8; 100:5); he is slow to anger, longsuffering, merciful, forgiving, and rich in love (Num. 14:18; Ps. 145:8); vengeance is his, he will repay (Deut. 32:35; cf. Prov. 24:17–20). We are coming into an hour when those who know and trust the Lord will see his goodness. Those who don't, will face the power of his wrath.

Lord, I want to know and trust you. Even in times of trouble, you shine a ray of hope into my life.

HABAKKUK

Habakkuk 2:2–3

And the L ORD answered me, and said, Write the vision, and make it plain upon tables, that he may run that readeth it. For the vision is yet for an appointed time, but at the end it shall speak, and not lie: though it tarry, wait for it; because it will surely come, it will not tarry.

This book is unique because it is conversational. Habakkuk was disturbed by the wickedness prevalent during the reign of Jehoiakim. The king was notoriously wicked: he was covetous, he shed innocent blood, and he oppressed the people (Jer. 22:13–29). When confronted by a prophecy of Urijah, Jehoiakim issued a warrant for the prophet's arrest, chased him into Egypt where he had fled, and brought him back to Judah for execution (Jer. 26:20–23). When a scribe read the scroll of Jeremiah in the presence of Jehoiakim, the king snatched it, slashed it with a penknife, and threw it into the fire (Jer. 36:23).

Habakkuk's first question to God was "How long must we suffer this wickedness?" The first thing God told Habakkuk was to write down his vision and publish it. Then he said that the proud, arrogant, and those full of falsehood would die. The people in right relationship with God would survive because they performed the Lord's will faithfully every day.

Do you have a vision for your life? If the answer is yes, what is it? Do you have it written somewhere? Can you look back to it in the times when vision and purpose seem to be gone? We need personal vision for our life.

The Bible declares that the vision he gives you is for an appointed time. When you have vision and you live that vision, God will fulfill it in his time.

Create a plan for your life. Pray about it. Involve your pastor and mentors. For when you write the vision and make it plain, God will make it come to pass.

Lord, give me personal vision for my life. Help me to make it plain and follow it. And I know that you will bring it to pass in your time.

Habakkuk 2:14
*For the earth shall be filled with the knowledge of the glory of the L*ORD*, as the waters cover the sea.*

This is our mission: that the whole earth be filled with the glory of the Lord. Pray for it. Act out the mission. It is the will of God.

Lord, let the whole earth be filled with your glory!

Habakkuk 3:2
*O L*ORD*, I have heard thy speech, and was afraid: O L*ORD*, revive thy work in the midst of the years, in the midst of the years make known; in wrath remember mercy.*

"As he meditated on God's work in human affairs, Habakkuk was overcome with an awe-inspiring sense of the greatness of the Lord.
. . . He prayed for God's renewed involvement in Israel" (Nelson Study Bible).

When God convicts us of wrongdoing, it is awe inspiring and a bit scary. We realize we have messed up. We either have neglected to do things we should have done, or we've done things we weren't supposed to do. But Habakkuk declared to the Lord, "Revive thy work in the midst of the years." When it seems like we are broken and messed up, this should be our prayer.

Lord, thank you for showing me what I did wrong. I repent before you. Even though I've gone astray, revive your work in me, Lord.

ZEPHANIAH

Zephaniah 1:14–16

The great day of the Lord is near, it is near, and hasteth greatly, even the voice of the day of the Lord: the mighty man shall cry there bitterly. That day is a day of wrath, a day of trouble and distress, a day of wasteness and desolation, a day of darkness and gloominess, a day of clouds and thick darkness, a day of the trumpet and alarm against the fenced cities, and against the high towers.

Zephaniah prophesied during the reign of Josiah, king of Judah. The theme of his book is the "day of the Lord." Instead of predicting judgment of this "day" on Assyria, as Joel had, Zephaniah predicted "the day of the Lord" (judgment) on Judah—the Babylonian invasion, the destruction of Jerusalem in 587 BC, and the subsequent exile. Even though the southern kingdom was approaching disaster, Zephaniah offered encouragement for Jerusalem and God's people concerning their future.

The "day of the Lord" is coming swiftly in our age as well. For some, the second coming of Christ will be the greatest day in the most wonderful sense. It will be the day they've been preparing for their entire lives. It will be the day they are raptured into the presence of God.

However, for others it will be a great day in the most terrible sense. A day when there shall be bitter crying, waste and desolation, darkness and gloom.

When that "great day" comes for you, how do you want it to be?

I pray I will be ready for the great day of your return, Jesus. I want to go to Heaven and bring as many people with me as possible.

Zephaniah 2:3
Seek ye the Lord, all ye meek of the earth, which have wrought his judgment; seek righteousness, seek meekness: it may be ye shall be hid in the day of the Lord's anger.

Lord, I will seek your righteousness and meekness in my life. Please hide me from disaster on "that day."

HAGGAI

Haggai 1:3–6

Then came the word of the Lord by Haggai the prophet, saying, Is it time for you, O ye, to dwell in your cieled houses, and this house lie waste? Now therefore thus saith the Lord of hosts; Consider your ways. Ye have sown much, and bring in little; ye eat, but ye have not enough; ye drink, but ye are not filled with drink; ye clothe you, but there is none warm; and he that earneth wages earneth wages to put it into a bag with holes.

Much of what is written in the series *The Road to Relationship* is about furthering your personal relationship with God. However, I'd like to use Haggai's message to provide some context to our relationship with the church.

After seventy years of exile, the new Persian Empire allowed the Jews to return to Jerusalem to rebuild the temple and the city. Unfortunately, after they had built the altar and part of the temple foundation, they found it more expedient to establish luxurious homes and businesses for themselves. The Jews had been in Palestine about fifteen years after their return when Haggai's ministry began. It is estimated that this prophet was in his eighties.

Haggai may have been old, but he put everything he had into the urgent message: "Consider your ways! You're working hard and getting nowhere! Get that temple built, and get it done in a hurry!"

Haggai's words remind us to put our focus on building up the church. We, especially in western culture, live in a "me society." Even the gospel becomes about us and increasing the blessings in our life. While there is a biblical tie to blessing, remember that we must be about our Father's business.

We cannot say we are living for God if we don't belong to a church. It is God's way. Give to your church your time, talent, and treasure, and God will bless you for it. In the midst of growth for yourself, make sure you are also involved in growing the church. Don't get so caught up in your own life that you miss what God is doing in the whole body of Christ.

Lord, help me to consider my ways. Let me be more concerned about adding growth to the church. Help me to edify—build up—your whole body and not just myself.

Haggai 1:13–14
Then spake Haggai the Lord's messenger in the Lord's message unto the people, saying, I am with you, saith the Lord. And the Lord stirred up the spirit of Zerubbabel the son of Shealtiel, governor of Judah, and the spirit of Joshua the son of Josedech, the high priest, and the spirit of all the remnant of the people; and they came and did work in the house of the Lord of hosts, their God.

Zerubbabel was of royal blood, being in the lineage of David, and therefore was an ancestor of Jesus Christ. He was instrumental in leading the returning exiles back to Jerusalem. After construction of the altar was completed, Zerubbabel had restored temple worship, but work on the temple structure had been neglected for nearly sixteen years. Haggai's preaching revived Zerubbabel's zeal for completing the temple, along with the high priest, and all the people, and the temple was completed.

The Spirit of God will flow through your leaders down to you. Getting with the flow is key. When Haggai the prophet thundered, "You can get that temple built because the Lord will be with you!" it stirred up the spirit of the leaders and they all came together to work on the temple.

Take note of this in your spiritual leaders. When they catch fresh vision, jump on board!

I will catch the zeal of my leaders and follow them in building up your church.

Haggai 2:7–9
And I will shake all nations, and the desire of all nations shall come: and I will fill this house with glory, saith the LORD of hosts. The silver is mine, and the gold is mine, saith the LORD of hosts. The glory of this latter house shall be greater than of the former, saith the LORD of hosts: and in this place will I give peace, saith the LORD of hosts.

When the elderly saw Zerubbabel's completed temple, they were disappointed. They remembered the majesty, the glittering splendor, and the treasures of Solomon's temple, and this new temple just didn't seem to measure up.

But Haggai relayed the Lord's message that the "latter house" would be greater than the "former house." They should not despise the result of their labors, for it was a tangible representation of God's faithfulness and fulfillment of past promises as well as a foreshadow of things to come. This latter temple would also be full of the wealth of the nations. After all, all the treasure of the earth belonged to God.

What a powerful prophecy of the last days! God will fill his house with glory. Everything belongs to him, and the glory of this latter house will be greater than the former. And in this place, he will give peace.

In these last days, God's glory is going to shine brighter than ever before. There may be trouble all around, but expect glory and peace to be more prevalent in the church than ever before.

Lord, fill my church with your glory. Fill the earth with your glory. Shake the nations of this world. Stir up our spirits in these last days, and let there be peace in our midst.

ZECHARIAH

Zechariah 3:7–8

Thus saith the L<small>ORD</small> of hosts; If thou wilt walk in my ways, and if thou wilt keep my charge, then thou shalt also judge my house, and shalt also keep my courts, and I will give thee places to walk among these that stand by. Hear now, O Joshua the high priest, thou, and thy fellows that sit before thee: for they are men wondered at: for, behold, I will bring forth my servant the BRANCH.

Zechariah prophesied in Jerusalem at the same time as Haggai, only Zechariah had been born in Babylon and was thus much younger. Zechariah was of priestly descent. His messages called for righteousness in home life, in the political arena, and in worship.

Zechariah had eight "night visions" in which he saw (1) a man among the myrtle trees, (2) four horns and four carpenters, (3) a measuring line, (4) a golden candlestick and two olive trees, (5) a flying scroll, (6) an ephah, and (7) four chariots with no horsemen. But the central vision of them all (3:1–10) was of Joshua, the high priest, dressed in dirty garments. Joshua was given clean garments and a clean turban with a golden plate that said, "HOLINESS TO THE LORD," symbolizing that Israel would once again have a priestly mediator.

"Branch" or "tender shoot" is a messianic title (Zech. 6:12; Isa. 4:1-6; 53:2; Jer. 23:5–7) that "speaks of a future permanent forgiveness the Messiah would accomplish when he comes to redeem the nation and to establish peace, prosperity, and security on the earth" (*Holman Illustrated Bible Dictionary*). Thus, Zechariah's central vision not only pertains to Joshua, the high priest, but it also is a prophecy of Jesus Christ, the Messiah, who will be both priest and king. He is the "Branch" that will restore the everlasting kingdom of David, and this Branch will be the foundation stone of the temple.

Jesus, you are both priest and king in my life! I praise you for who you are!

Zechariah 7:10

And oppress not the widow, nor the fatherless, the stranger, nor the poor; and let none of you imagine evil against his brother in your heart.

We are not to be so self-absorbed that we fail to notice what's going on outside the church walls. The Bible is full of commandments to help the widow, the fatherless, the stranger, and the poor. Pray that you can be a help to those downtrodden in life and who need a Savior!

God, I want to be a help to the widows, fatherless, strangers, outcast, downtrodden, depressed, and poor. Give me opportunity to spread your light today.

Zechariah 8:8–9

And I will bring them, and they shall dwell in the midst of Jerusalem: and they shall be my people, and I will be their God, in truth and in righteousness. Thus saith the LORD of hosts; Let your hands be strong, ye that hear in these days these words by the mouth of the prophets, which were in the day that the foundation of the house of the LORD of hosts was laid, that the temple might be built.

God gave his people a promise, then immediately declared, "Let your hands be strong!" What do you do when God speaks a promise into your life? You keep on working! Your situation may not immediately change just because you have a promise. So keep praying that your hands will be strong, and keep working until your promise comes to pass.

Make my hands strong in you, Jesus. After I receive my promise, I will work harder than ever to obtain it.

Zechariah 10:1
Ask ye of the LORD rain in the time of the latter rain; so the LORD shall make bright clouds, and give them showers of rain, to every one grass in the field.

We see rain as both a good thing and a bad thing in the Bible. Sometimes it is a sign of destruction; other times it is a sign of blessing. The rain in Zechariah 10:1 is a sign of restoration and blessing. Pray that the rain of

God's blessing and favor will fall on your life. And get ready. Because when God says it is going to rain, it will rain!

Lord, send the rain of blessing in my life. Form the clouds over me to pour out the rain of your redemption and favor.

Zechariah 13:9
And I will bring the third part through the fire, and will refine them as silver is refined, and will try them as gold is tried: they shall call on my name, and I will hear them: I will say, It is my people: and they shall say, The LORD is my God.

The refining process can be painful. You feel crushed, melted, bruised, broken, and battered. However, this process removes the impurities from your life. When God gets finished refining you, you will come out as pure silver and gold.

Sometimes God tries you even when you haven't done anything wrong. For instance, Job was living a godly life. He had committed no sin that needed to be repented of, because he offered daily sacrifices for himself and his family. Yet the Lord "tried" Job—put him through the refining process—not to remove sinful dross but to show that Job was pure gold (Job 23:10).

Lord, do whatever you have to do to refine me and remove any impurities from my life. I want to come forth as pure gold in your sight. In Jesus' name, amen.

Zechariah 14:6–7
And it shall come to pass in that day, that the light shall not be clear, nor dark: but it shall be one day which shall be known to the LORD, not day, nor night: but it shall come to pass, that at evening time it shall be light.

"At the evening time it shall be light." We are living in a world full of darkness. But Romans 5:20–21 says, "But where sin abounded, grace did much more abound: that as sin hath reigned unto death, even so might grace reign through righteousness unto eternal life by Jesus Christ our Lord."

There is no darkness so thick and wicked that God's grace cannot pierce through it like a laser beam. His light is bright and clear. It isn't sunlight; it is heavenly light.

Lord, be a shining light in my evening time. Bring light to this world in the midst of its darkness.

MALACHI

Malachi 2:2

If ye will not hear, and if ye will not lay it to heart, to give glory unto my name, saith the LORD of hosts, I will even send a curse upon you, and I will curse your blessings: yea, I have cursed them already, because ye do not lay it to heart.

Nothing is known of Malachi except for what his book reveals. Unlike Haggai and Zechariah, who are mentioned in Ezra 5:1 and 6:14, Malachi is not mentioned anywhere else in the Bible. His name means "My Messenger." He most likely prophesied in the post-exilic period between 515 and 458 BC.

Rather than demanding that the Jews honor him, Jehovah instead asked why sons honored their fathers and servants honored their masters, but the people did not honor their Lord and Father. The people lacked understanding and continually questioned and argued with God.

The excitement generated by the preaching of Haggai and Zechariah had long since dissipated. The temple was rebuilt and worship established, but social and religious problems still plagued the nation.

The Lord called for the people to mend their ways. They should honor the Lord's name by bringing pure offerings, being faithful to their covenants—both to God and to their spouse—and by bringing their tithes. If the priests didn't alter their behavior, God would curse them and remove them from their ministry.

The lesson for us is that we do not argue with God. He is sovereign. He is holy. He is mighty. When he speaks, we listen. It is that simple.

Lord, when you speak to me about changes I need to make in my life, whether your message comes through prayer, the word, or my pastor, I will make that change. I will not argue with you.

Malachi 3:8–10

Will a man rob God? Yet ye have robbed me. But ye say, Wherein have we robbed thee? In tithes and offerings. Ye are cursed with a curse: for ye have robbed me, even this whole nation. Bring ye all the tithes into the storehouse, that there may be meat in mine house, and prove me now herewith, saith the Lord of hosts, if I will not open you the windows of heaven, and pour you out a blessing, that there shall not be room enough to receive it.

God's law is simple. If you don't follow his commandments, you cannot expect a good outcome at the end of your life. If you do obey his commandments, however, God will pour out more blessings on you than you have the capacity to receive.

In the above passage, Malachi addressed the subject of tithing. Tithing is a biblical principle beginning with Abraham and continuing into the New Testament era. We are to give to the Lord a tenth of our increase. He requires the "firstfruits," which for us would mean that as soon as we are paid, we give God his tithe. We don't wait until we've paid every bill and bought whatever else we want before checking to see if there's enough left over for God at the end of the month.

This commandment about tithing comes with permission for us to "try" God. He is saying, "Do you find it hard to believe that after giving me a tenth you won't have enough? Just try me and see. I'll make good my promise; I'll give you more in return than you can contain."

For the Jews, these blessings came in many different forms: God promised that he would guard their crops from insects and disease, resulting in abundant yields, and their grapes would not fall from the vines before they were ripe (3:11, NLT). For us, these blessings could be a new job, a raise, an unexpected gift, a car that needs less repairs, good health and healing so that we require fewer medical visits, and so on.

This commandment not only comes with permission to "try" God; it also comes with a curse if you do not render the tithe to God. One aspect of the curse is that you are cutting off the flow of God's blessings by withholding your tithe. In fact, God views it as robbery.

So go ahead and try him. If you will give to God first, he will bless you. It is guaranteed.

Lord, I will give you what belongs to you. I don't want to live cursed, but I choose to live in your overflowing blessings.

Malachi 3:16–17
Then they that feared the LORD spake often one to another: and the LORD hearkened, and heard it, and a book of remembrance was written before him for them that feared the LORD, and that thought upon his name. And they shall be mine, saith the LORD of hosts, in that day when I make up my jewels; and I will spare them, as a man spareth his own son that serveth him.

Malachi is the last book of the Old Testament. No more prophets were sent by God until John the Baptist stepped on the scene urging the people to prepare the way of the Lord. (See Isaiah 40:3–5; Luke 1:11–17.)

No matter how wicked a nation is, there will always be some who fear the Lord. Judah was an example of this. The NIV says, "Those who feared the LORD talked with each other, and the LORD listened and heard. A scroll of remembrance was written in his presence concerning those who feared the LORD and honored his name" (v. 16). To God's ears, conversations like these sound like a prayer. The Lord calls his people his "treasured possession." He will have compassion on them and spare them and protect them.

Zechariah 2:8 says, "He that toucheth you touches the apple of his eye." The apple of the eye refers to the pupil, "a delicate part of the eye that is essential for vision and that therefore must be protected at all costs" (NIV Study Bible). The Lord will protect his people, his treasured possession!

Jesus, I give glory and honor to you. Thank you for listening and bestowing blessing and protection on us as we talk with others about you. Praise your holy name!

Made in the USA
Columbia, SC
28 March 2024